An Old California Family

THE SOTOS OF CAMBRIA

ROBERT "BOBBY" SOTO

COPYRIGHT © 2011

BY ROBERT SOTO

ALL RIGHTS RESERVED

No part of this work may be reproduced or transmitted in any form or by any means, electronic or mechanical, including photocopying, recording, or by any information storage retrieval system without the written permission of the author, except by a reviewer who may quote short passages.

ISBN: 978-1-930401-8-60
Third Printing 2014

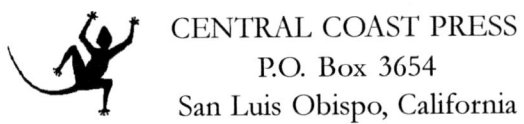

CENTRAL COAST PRESS
P.O. Box 3654
San Luis Obispo, California

Library of Congress Control Number: 2014936123

Back cover text by Taylor Coffman
Back cover painting by Al Riesau

DEDICATION

I dedicate this book to the memory of my great-grandfather Cipriano Soto. The Soto family established itself in the Cambria area largely because of the commitment of my great-grandparents Cipriano and Carmel Soto. The hardships they endured after purchasing the upper home ranch on a meager workingman's salary allowed the Soto family to flourish on the Central Coast around the Cambria-San Simeon area. Their beloved land was always considered home to our entire family. Cipriano loved his family so greatly that he relinquished living on his own property so his sons could live and work the land. Cipriano, as pictured in 1948 on the cover, will always be etched in my memory as more than a great-grandfather. He was also a family hero and patriarch.

Robert and Shirlene; 2006

I also dedicate this book to the memory of my beloved sister, Shirlene Ann Soto, who was so supportive of this effort. She was highly trained and educated as a historian, and she was truly excited to assist me in documenting family stories. She often praised my recordings of family information and thought it critical to the family's future. Shirlene's tragic and premature death in 2009 was a shock to our entire family, an event that reinforced life's uncertainty.

Robert Soto

Courtesy: Carol (Soto) Lowry

1906 Soto Family Gathering at Dry Bones Homestead

(Sitting—from left) Andrew Soto, Ben Cooksey (son of Clara Asebez), Arthur Terrill (little boy), Edward Terrill (big boy)

(Sitting on chair—from left) Joaquin "Jack" Soto (fiddle), Anastacio Asebez (fiddle), Louisa "Beva" Soto (guitar), ? (head down)

(Standing—from left) Elmer Cooksey (married to Clara Asebez), Josefa (Asebez) Terrill, Clara (Asebez) Cooksey, Barney Soto, Archie Soto, Carmel (Asebez) Soto, Evelyn Soto (young child), Cipriano Soto, Joe Soto, ? (tall man), General Soto (in shadows), Dolores (Grajalva) Soto

CONTENTS

Dedication 3
Contents 5
List of Photos 6
Foreword by Taylor Coffman 8
Preface 10
Introduction: Soto Family Heritage 12
GENERATION 1 (YGNACIO) 22
GENERATION 2 (ISIDORO) 29
    Appendix I Encounter between Miller and Vasquez 38
    Appendix II "1819 – A Bear Hunt" 39
GENERATION 3 (LAZARO) 45
    Appendix III Soto Monterey Adobes 51
    Appendix IV Don Rafael Soto 57
    Appendix V The Last Will and Testament of Rafael Soto, 1839 61
    Appendix VI The Last Will and Testament of Joaquin Soto, 1852 ... 64
GENERATION 4 (GENERAL) 66
    Appendix VII Dry Bones 80
GENERATION 5 (CIPRIANO) 86
    Appendix VIII Edwin Terrill's Accident 119
    Appendix IX Jack Soto 121
GENERATION 6 (ERNEST) 125
GENERATION 7 (VERNON) 141
GENERATION 8 (ROBERT) 163
    Appendix X Soto Family Tree 171
GENERATION 9 (MONTE) 173
GENERATION 10 (RHETT) 177
Summary 179
Bibliography 182
Index 186

LIST OF PHOTOS

Robert and Shirlene; 2006 3
1906 Soto Family Gathering at Dry Bones Homestead 4
Royal Presidio of San Ignacio de Tubac; circa 1774 16
1775-76 Anza Expedition Overland Route 21
Vasquez-Cantua-Soto Family Tree 31
Map of Joaquin Soto's Rancho El Piojo 47
Native Montereyans 52
The Historic Soto Adobe 54
Soto-Greer House (Palo Alto); circa 1940 60
General Soto as a young man 66
Grant Deed to Natoma Campfire Girls 72
1933-34 Property Tax Bill from Dry Bones 73
Vernon Soto with Ernest (top photo) and Elsie (bottom photo) at Dry
  Bones Adobe; 1936 74
San Antonio Band members standing in front of Cambria's Ridgon Hall; circa 1906 77
General's 1850 Colt .36 caliber 5-shot Revolver Pistol 78
Cipriano Soto mounted on his horse 86
Asebez Family; 1884 87
Family Cowboys at Dry Bones Homestead 88
Cipriano's and Carmel's Signatures 89
Cipriano's Handwritten Notes of Places Lived 90
1910 Deed from Carpenter and Ivins to Ed Asebez and Cipriano Soto 92
1925 Deed from Asebez to Ernest and Andrew Soto 93
Barn "Dad" Ingles built at Home Ranch; circa 1970s 95
Cipriano, Andrew and Arthur Terrill on hay wagon at Home Ranch 97
Margaret (Ingles) Soto being lifted onto San Simeon pier; 1900 99
Soto family climbing over grade to visit Dry Bones Homestead; 1906 100
Barney Soto roping calves at Hearst Ranch 102
Young "Pico" and Edwin Soto with Cambria School in background 103
Carmel Soto in yard at Home Ranch with steep sidehill in background; circa 1920 105
Cipriano Soto riding horseback in early Cambria Parade; circa 1940s 107
Cipriano Soto, Grand Marshall of SLO La Fiesta de las Flores Parade; 1948 108
Don "Pancho" Estrada with Augustine "Gus" Soto, San Simeon Beach 110
Obie and Newell Terrill, Vernon and Snow Soto on San Simeon house porch with
  Cipriano; circa 1929 111
Newspaper article of Carmel and Cipriano's 50th Wedding Anniversary; 1945 113
Cipriano and Carmel Soto's 50th Wedding Party, Green Valley; 1945 114
Rafael Mora 114
Lila Soto with Soto's Market delivery truck; 1936 115
Margaret "Dolly" and Joaquin Jr. "Pico" Soto 116
Youngest daughter, Betty (Soto) Williams; 1930 116
Soto family picnic in Cayucos; early 1940s 118
Joaquin "Jack" Soto, Grand Marshall of SLO La Fiesta de las Flores; 1951 121

Jack's wife, Agnes (Maggetti) Soto, making tortillas 122
Young Ernest Soto on horseback at Summers Ranch; circa 1930s 125
Letter regarding payment to Soto Brother's for firewood 128
Young Archie and Ernest Soto all "dressed up" in early 1920s 129
Ernest Soto (on Loco), 1973 Grand Marshall of Cambria Pinedorado 131
Elsie and Ernest Soto; 1975 132
Buffum house; 1870s 133
Home of Robert and Debbie Soto 133
Elsie (Barlogio) Soto; 1906 134
George "Chap" Soto horseback as a young man 135
George Soto with "Miss Tuesday" at Elsie Soto Ranch; 1960 136
Lehman house high up in the Mountains of Santa Rosa Creek; circa 1920s 138
Neighboring ranchers at the "Lehman" Ranch; 1930s 139
Elsie Soto and Vernon, on raft at Dry Bones; 1935 140
Vernon Soto on horseback at upper Summers Ranch; 1945 141
Cipriano with grandson Jim Soto, up the Coast on the Hearst Ranch; 1943 144
Vernon and Carol (Soto) Lowry coon hunting at old Summers house; circa 1937 145
Early-day Cambria Rodeo at Phelan Grove; circa 1930 147
Pamphlet from Cambria Rodeo held at Phelan's Grove; 1935 148
Early-day Cambria Rodeo Grounds; circa 1940s 149
Cambria Rodeo float, San Luis Obispo La Fiesta de las Flores Parade; 1948 149
Vernon and Althea Soto, Summers Ranch; 1946 150
Neighbor Olympio Fiscalini, Santa Rosa Creek, beneath the swinging bridge; 1940 151
Snow, Steven, Bonnie, Andrew and Cipriano, Rotanzi Ranch; 1952 152
How Wong's house next to Pacific Ocean 153
Ed and Lucy Kester, 50th Wedding Anniversary, Smithers Ranch; early 1950s 156
Ervin, Lester "Dutch," Althea "Polly," and Shirley Smithers, Smithers Ranch; 1934 157
Cambria "Rosie the Riveters" 158
Footbridge crossing Santa Rosa Creek, Cambria 159
Althea Smithers, Coast Union High School; 1944 160
Vernon and Shirlene riding in the 1953 Pinedorado Parade 162
Robert Soto roping calves, El Monte Ranch; 1991 163
Three-year-old Robert "Bobby" roping his first calf at the Lehman Ranch; 1953 164
Debbie, Melissa, Robert and Monte, El Monte Ranch; 1985 167
Soto Family tree, page 1 171
Soto Family tree, page 2 172
Monte Soto horseback (on Rojo) at Home Ranch; 2001 173
Beautiful bride Melissa at garden wedding; 2006 176
Monte and Rhett on Derby 177
Mackenzie, Melissa and Alina 178

FOREWORD

I've long wanted to write a book about Cambria, one that would be worthy of everybody in the local pantheon, past and present. Now I don't have to. Instead, Bobby Soto has done it, and he's done it exceptionally well.

I didn't know that his heritage traced back as far as the Anza expeditions of 1774 and of 1775-1776. But then I learned that Bobby didn't know this either—until he got into his research in great detail. That's the fun of his book: finding out all these new things about Cambria and other places close by, like Adelaida and San Simeon and San Carpojo, a rugged canyon up the coast from Piedras Blancas. Its proper name is San Carpoforo, and yet "San Carpojo" is what the natives call it; and thus do we follow suit in the pages of this book.

Bobby and I have San Simeon and Hearst Castle in common. We knew each other when we worked on "the hill" several years ago, although we didn't know each other well. Now we do, thanks to his book, which I've had the honor of reading and fine-tuning for publication. It's one of the best editorial jobs I've ever had. I've loved gaining new knowledge from it, and I've enjoyed seeing how Bobby presents his facts and findings. He has a writer's makeup, a historian's knack, no question about it.

With my own family, I can trace things back to 1806. That's when a certain Michael Coffman was born in Virginia. In contrast, Bobby's story goes back at least thirty years before that—back to the time of the American Revolution on the eastern seaboard, when California was still a land of mystery and uncertain promise. There may even have been forebears of his in the two Portola expeditions of 1769 and 1770. Bobby isn't sure, though, and he doesn't stretch the point in favor of those events. Being a known descendant of the Anza expeditions is antiquarian enough.

I was just a kid, twenty years old, when I moved to Cambria in 1970. One of my first jobs downtown—East Village to latter-day folk—was at Otto's Chevron on Main Street. Nearly the whole town stopped there for gas, and many of the people had charge accounts. Thus did I learn their names and get to know them as locals, who were often from old families like the Sotos and the Fiscalinis. Those people always trusted me—I wasn't sure why—as though I were native-born. I was impressed, and I was mighty glad. Vernon Soto, Bobby's dad, was one who looked me straight in the eye with respect and warmth, as though I'd always been around. Vernon's wife, Polly (Bobby's mother), worked at the Cambria Grammar School. She and my wife, Janis, who worked at the school in 1971 and '72, became friends. Our status as locals gained stature and momentum. Later, Janis ran a school of dance downtown; one of her students was Bobby and

Debbie Soto's young daughter, Melissa.

And then there was Soto's Market, where we Coffmans always shopped; we were never Cookie Crock people, as I explained to Bobby when we started this project. At Soto's, Wilfred Lyons and his wife, Hazel, treated us like locals, the same as the customers at Otto's Chevron had. Pico Soto was there too, and so was his youngest sister, Betty Williams. Betty called our first-born daughter "Somie," which wasn't very close to "Simone," but no matter. We were locals through and through, so far as Betty and Wilfred and the others were concerned. Our two daughters were accepted and embraced in the same way. I'll never forget when Betty drove down to Moonstone Beach one day in 1971 to watch me surf: I'd shown up in the market often enough in my damp wetsuit—this was before there were many surfers in town—and she wanted to see what in the world it was all about. I'll never forget the sight: Betty standing on the cliff in her khaki Soto's Market shop coat, hands at her hips, squinting as she looked out to sea—and seeing me, waiting for a wave.

Bobby's book is full of stories, good stories all of them. It's full of facts, too, facts and events that we've had far too little of for years now. Geneva Hamilton's book, *Where the Highway Ends*, appeared in 1974. We Cambrians and other lovers of local history have been making do with that book almost exclusively ever since. Here's an alternative finally, at long last. Read it and be transported back to the North Coast and the Cambria area of the late 1800s and the early 1900s, and to the Cambria of recent decades as well. Bobby has tapped a gold mine of nostalgia and history, of genealogy and local color, all of it organized around the simple principle of "generations," of which he himself is Generation 8. If I think back to that paternal grandmother of mine, I'm Generation 5. Bobby and his fellow Sotos have got me pretty well beat. And they'll have most everyone else beat while they're at it. As if the Anza expeditions weren't ancient enough, Bobby can take the Soto story back as far as northern Spain, near the Basque country, in the seventeenth century.

It's all in this book, and everything's told in a way that will leave you hungry for more. I had the pleasure of suggesting a title for the book. I didn't hesitate a minute in saying *An Old California Family: The Sotos of Cambria*, which Bobby applauded. The Cambria I escaped to from Los Angeles in 1970 is mostly a distant memory, but I'll always have his book to remind me of what drew me to the place to begin with. I'm glad I came. And I'm glad to have him and his fellow Sotos as my guides, all these years later.

Taylor Coffman
San Luis Obispo

PREFACE

The writing of this book has been a task of total enjoyment. Typically as one matures, one begins to look back and yearn for more family stories and memories. I have often wished that my grandfather had written down his family stories, only to realize that someday my grandchildren might desire the same thing. It soon became apparent that it was my responsibility to document these stories for future generations, and it was far too late to capitalize on lost opportunities.

Fortunately, the Soto family remained in one place, Cambria, for many generations, thus limiting the loss of artifacts and photos. Although family dynamics have changed throughout the generations, the core interest and love of family history continues to flow through the veins of this pioneering family.

Good health has also played an important role in the success of this family. Many elderly Soto family members remained active, with sharp keen minds, well into their seventies, eighties, and even nineties. Their memories of "the good old days" always amazed me, and without these recollections there would be no book. Those good old days were of a more simple life, yet they were also of a time when family relationships were highly valued and appreciated. There was no escape to nightly television, no Internet, but only the good times of people enjoying each other's company, with music, stories and memories being the main entertainment.

Stories and photographs from the collection of Cipriano Soto, Margaret "Dolly" Soto, Joaquin "Jack" Soto, Vernon Soto, Althea Soto, Andrew "Snow" Soto, Ernest Soto, Elsie Soto, Jim Soto, Carol (Soto) Lowry, Karen (Soto) Snow, Steven Soto, Shirlene Soto, Newell Terrill, and from my own collection were used throughout this book. The Cambria Historical Society was also very helpful in providing documents for this publication. My thanks go to Katie and Monte Soto for their computer assistance. My cousin Milene Radford's keen eyes greatly assisted in correcting overlooked grammatical errors. The work of Melissa (Soto) Carstairs was also essential in proofreading the rough drafts. The expertise of editor Taylor Coffman was critical in publishing a quality document. A special thanks to Bill Strasen for his drawings. The readers: Robert Pavlik, Carole Adams and Karen (Soto) Snow, also greatly contributed to this document. I want to thank my late sister, Shirlene Soto, a historian, for her assistance in editing and for ideas on how to improve this book. I especially want to thank my wife, Debbie Soto, for her encouragement throughout the writing process. Debbie's constant trips to the library for research material were greatly appreciated.

In compiling the information, family stories, and history for this book, I soon understood how greatly the Soto family contributed to the history of Alta California. The Sotos were generally non-political and preferred to live a quiet rural life; however, the intertwined relatives and progeny of this large family made a huge impact on shaping early California. Because of the limited possibilities of finding spouses in Alta California, many of the Anza expedition families married within this pioneering group. This resulted in a tightly knit group of settlers determined to make a successful transition in their new world. The Soto family was related to many of the first political families of California with surnames like Castro, Vallejo, Osio, Vasquez, Lugo, and Garcia. It was only after this realization that I fully grasped that by documenting family stories, the early history of California was also being recorded.

In writing this book, I began to recognize that this was an evolving piece of history, with each new piece of information adding to the total picture of the Soto family. As small pieces of research became available, the "holes" of history slowly began to be filled. I soon realized there would never be a completely satisfactory moment to end this book, as new information continued to fall into my hands. I finally came to the realization that it was necessary to publish this document "as is." I'm hopeful that future generations will add information and provide a more complete understanding of the Soto family in early California.

This book is not intended for use solely as a historical document but rather as a collection of family stories, preserved for history. I'm grateful to the many family members for taking their time to share their recollections with me. Now these recollections are recorded for posterity.

INTRODUCTION: SOTO FAMILY HERITAGE

Much of the Soto family history is based on information gathered by family members and on their personal recollections. My cousin Newell Terrill has greatly contributed to this effort by painstakingly gathering information on the lineage of the Soto family. Newell continues his extensive research on the Soto family from California mission-system records and historical documents. It should be pointed out that some confusion exists because the spelling of Spanish names is often translated differently for the same person (for example, Ygnacio vs. Ignacio). Adding further complexity, the Spanish culture often lists identical first names with only the middle names appearing differently. The spelling of some names changed over generations, such as Asebez, which around 1900 changed to Asabez. Also, as mentioned by Don Garate, noted author and expert on Juan Bautista de Anza, that explorer is properly identified as Anza, not de Anza. Because of this, I have consistently identified him as Anza unless listing his full name.

This book is organized by male family lineage, beginning with Ygnacio Soto as Generation 1. A list of children follows each generation and **bold type** is used to identify my own direct lineage. The list of children has been omitted beginning with generation 7 for purposes of safeguarding the personal information of those currently living.

The earliest Sotos (or more accurately *de Sotos*) came from Spain and have been traced back to the early 1600s. Information from Ancestry.com suggests that the first de Sotos originated in Spain's La Rioja region; localities included Anguiano, Logrono, and Rincon de Soto.

When the Roman troops arrived nearly two centuries before Christ, La Rioja was mostly occupied by Celts. This area was later invaded by Arabs, beginning in the eighth century. It is this influence of Arab culture and Christian repopulation that gives the unique identity to La Rioja. Finally, in 1177, King Henry I of England favored the Kingdom of Castile in an ongoing dispute. For centuries, disagreement continued over La Rioja until Henry IV again claimed the region for Castile in the late 1500s.

During the Peninsular War (1808–1814), La Rioja was taken by the Napoleonic French forces and was not recovered until 1814. The decision declaring La Rioja to be an independent province occurred with the Constitution of 1812. In November 1833, after continuing disputes, a

Royal Decree outlined a smaller border of La Rioja that has remained unchanged to the present time.

Although the information is sketchy, Juan Nicolas de Soto, born in the La Rioja region on July 11, 1639, is identified as the first traceable Soto. Two generations later another Juan Nicolas de Soto (b. 1690) and his wife, Maria Juliana de Avila, are listed as living in Sinaloa, New Spain. Their son, Ygnacio de Soto (the *de* was dropped when the family came to Alta California), and his wife, Maria Barbara Espinosa, along with their son, Jose Antonio, and daughter, Maria Francisca, were selected by Juan Bautista de Anza to accompany the group to settle Alta California in 1775. Ygnacio became a soldier who, along with his son Francisco and grandson Antonio, served in the military at the Presidio of San Francisco. Thus, the Soto beginnings in Alta California were that of a military family.

A brief history may help to understand Ygnacio Soto's decision to leave his family in Sinaloa and make the dangerous trip into the vastly unknown Alta California. The Spaniards occupied present-day Mexico from 1521 through 1821 and referred to it as New Spain. Only after Mexican independence in 1821 was it called Mexico.

Culiacan was established in northwest New Spain by 1532, only a decade after the Aztec capital they conquered became Mexico City. From this point, however, the frontier didn't advance significantly towards the northwest. Spanish efforts to expand northward into Sonora in the early 1600s failed largely because of the resistance of the Yaquis Indians. This tribe fiercely fought any attempts to move into their domain.

After the founding of Villa Sinaloa, which boasted a garrison of twenty or more soldiers, the northern frontier took a dramatic move northward and to the east of Sinaloa. A peace agreement with the Indians was finally reached and Jesuit priests were permitted to establish missions at some villages in the early 1600s. In the mid-1600s, gold and silver were discovered in several areas, an event that brought the arrival of many miners.

Spain employed three critical institutions in establishing domination of the northwest frontier: the mission (church), the presidio (fort), and the pueblo (community). Northward expansion was slow but continued into the 1700s. Several Indian uprisings occurred during this time, halting further significant advancement.

Sweeping changes finally came when Jose de Galvez was appointed "Visitador" (Royal Inspector) to New Spain. De Galvez was sent to reform

New Spain's financial, military, and governmental operation. He is credited with Spain's decision to advance northward.

In 1769, Jose de Galvez ordered the further occupation of Baja California and that of Alta California. His original plan for Alta California called for one presidio and five missions. The main presidio and one of the missions would be situated at Monterey, one of the missions at San Diego, with the three other missions connecting the two points. The Franciscans would be in charge of the new establishments. The advantage of utilizing the Franciscans was their availability, since they had recently replaced the Jesuits in Baja California.

In 1769-70, Alta California expeditions by land and sea established Mission San Diego, the Presidio of Monterey, and nearby Mission San Carlos Borromeo in Carmel. Three more missions were called for under the Galvez plan, two being established in 1771—San Antonio and San Gabriel (Los Angeles). Exploration of the Alta California coast in 1769 also established the existence of San Francisco Bay. Alta California was now considered a rich treasure for Spain, and it required protection. Moreover, the Spaniards realized that something must be done to occupy Alta California due to Russian encroachment from the north and the potential for general European intrusion into this promising land.

One significant reason that early colonists were willing to risk the difficult expedition into Alta California may have been the flood of 1770. This is reported to have left hundreds, perhaps thousands, homeless, especially in Sinaloa and southern Sonora. Villa Sinaloa was badly damaged by this flood. The old Jesuit church was swept away during these torrential storms, leaving only its belfry. Hundreds of homes were flooded; this may have been on the minds of colonists when making the drastic life-changing decision of whether or not to leave their homeland.

Juan Bautista de Anza, who came from a distinguished line of frontier soldiers, led one of the first land expeditions to Alta California. His father, also named Juan Bautista de Anza, had served twenty years as a captain in the Spanish army before his death in 1739. He was killed in a battle with the Apache Indians when young Anza was only a year old. It is assumed that young Anza received the best schooling possible for this time and area. In 1760, Anza made the rank of captain and was placed in command of the Presidio of Tubac (in present-day Arizona). This placed young Anza in a position to promote northern expansion.

In 1769, part of the expedition under the Spanish explorer Gaspar de Portola and Father Junipero Serra, Franciscan president of the California Mission system, was by land. They marched through the dry, arid terrain of Baja California, a highly undesirable route. The other portion of the party came by sea and experienced severe storms and numerous other difficulties. In Harry Crosby's *Gateway to Alta California* (2003), a list of explorers present in San Diego in July 1769 identifies two Sotos—Alejandro de Soto and Mateo Ignacio de Soto. Alejandro (b. 1745 in El Fuerte, Sinaloa) is identified as going north from San Diego to Monterey with Portola in 1770 on his second search for Monterey Bay (the first exploration in 1769 was unsuccessful since Portola was unable to locate Monterey Bay). Alejandro remained in Monterey under the command of Pedro Fages.

Mateo de Soto was a soldier at the Presidio of San Diego in 1770. He was accused, along with two other soldiers, of attacking two young Indian girls near Mission San Diego. When charges were pressed, Mateo was away carrying mail to the Baja peninsula. It was assumed that Mateo learned of these charges, inasmuch as efforts to find him were fruitless and he fled to the mainland (present-day Mexico). Eventually, all three accused soldiers were "sentenced" to become settlers in Alta California pueblos. Mateo was not mentioned again in any historical records. I note this only to demonstrate that there were also Sotos on the two Portola expeditions of 1769 and 1770. However, the relationship of our family to either Alejandro or Mateo is unknown.

Due to the difficulties encountered by Portola, Father Serra traveled to Mexico City in 1773 to discuss other possible land routes into Alta California. In September 1773, Viceroy Bucarelli directed Anza to undertake an expedition to discover a new land route into this vast unknown territory.

On January 8, 1774, Anza and his party set out from the Presidio of Tubac with a total of thirty-four persons. They had thirty-five pack loads of provisions and sixty-five head of cattle for food. The sole purpose of this expedition was to discover a new overland route into Alta California. With the help of native Indian guides, Mission San Gabriel was reached on March 26, 1774. Although forged through extremely rough and rugged terrain, a new land route from Sonora to Alta California had now been discovered. Anza quickly retraced his route back to Tubac to spread the good news.

Courtesy: Bill Strasen

Royal Presidio of San Ignacio de Tubac; circa 1774

In December 1774, Anza accepted a new assignment to return over this same land route to establish new missions and settlements in Alta California. The second Anza expedition of 1775-76 was important because this was the first major attempt of the Spanish government to bring families into Alta California.

California's new governor, Felipe de Neve, had plans for expansion of troops along with the addition of colonists. This is not what Father Serra wanted. Serra told Governor de Neve that it was impossible to provide as much food from the mission granaries as de Neve wanted for his troops. De Neve resolved to place a farming colony in California to feed his army. This set the stage for the second expedition led by young Juan Bautista de Anza, who set out from Sonora for Alta California by land in September 1775. Some of the families recruited for this trip were intended for the new presidio at San Francisco (such as Ygnacio de Soto) while others were slated for the farming colony in present-day San Jose.

In the 1775-76 expedition, de Neve and Anza had added some two hundred persons to California, more than double the number of colonists in the province. Prior to 1774, there had been no Spanish women in the colony. A few came by sea in March 1774 and a few more followed in September. By January 1775, some soldiers had married California Indian women, and the total number of colonists was around 170.

Vladimir Guerrero, in *The Anza Trail and the Settling of California* (2006), demonstrates the critical importance of this colonizing attempt:

> The Anza expeditions of 1774 and 1776 constitute a little-known chapter in American history – the story of an immigrant group that established the character of California as much as the Puritans determined that of New England. Even though these settlers were in the service of the crown, they, like most immigrants, came by their own choosing, motivated by the prospect of a better life for themselves and their families. To achieve that in a distant and unknown land, they had the will and courage to undertake a voyage as long and difficult as any Atlantic crossing. Whether mestizo, white, indigenous, or black, they were a close-knit society with strong cultural and religious ties. As Spanish subjects relocating within their domains, they remained loyal to their king. It was only seventy-five years later [after 1848], with Spain and England expelled from the American mainland, that the United States in its westward expansion came to them, and these immigrants—assuming the name of "Californios"—took their place in American history.

Life was very difficult for Ygnacio de Soto while living in Sinaloa. It was a dry climate, and growing crops was backbreaking work. When the de Sotos were selected to travel overland to California, it must have been exciting yet humbling, for everything and everyone they knew would be left behind, including all their extended family. To entice them into making the trip, they were given clothes and new shoes (even ribbons for the little girls' hair). The women were issued chemises, white petticoats of Puebla cotton, hats, and varas of ribbons. The men were issued carbines, swords and lances, as well as heavy leather jackets for protection.

Frances Conley states in the book *Long Road to Rancho San Pablo* (1989):

> Recruitment for such an expedition was not easy. The men who enlisted would have to take their families on a fifteen hundred mile march across the deserts of northern Mexico, through the lands of the warlike Apaches, and up the almost unknown coast of California to the bay of San Francisco,

where no Spaniard had ever lived. It would mean permanent exile from family and friends, and since almost none of them could read and write, there would be no letters from home: to those left behind they would have died.

In 1773, Captain Fernando de Rivera was appointed Military Governor of Alta California and relocated to Monterey. A handful of early settlers moved with Rivera into Alta California, which allowed the Spaniard to explore the region.

In 1774, Captain Rivera explored the San Francisco area to select sites for future settlements. Although this preliminary expedition was successful, nearly two years would pass before Anza's colonists would eventually settle in San Francisco. This was largely due to Captain Rivera being unable to spare any additional soldiers for the founding of the new posts.

Early historical records show Ygnacio de Soto (age twenty-seven), his wife, Barbara de Espinosa (de Lugo) (age eighteen), and two children, Jose Antonio (age two) and Maria Francisca (age one), as being selected for the second Anza trip. Ygnacio was recruited by Anza on April 13, 1775. According to Marie Northrop in *Spanish-Mexican Families of Early California: 1769 – 1850* (1986), Barbara de Espinosa was a sister of another soldier, Francisco Salvador de Lugo, whose daughter, Maria Antonia Isabela de Lugo, became the mother of General Mariano de Guadalupe Vallejo. (General Vallejo was the highest military officer in Alta California and instrumental in its beginnings.) Francisco de Lugo came with the first families who were recruited by Captain Rivera in September of 1774. Also accompanying Anza was Juan Francisco Bernal, a mestizo from Rancho del Tule (Sonora), age fifty-three, and his wife, Maria Josefa (de Soto) Bernal (an Española, age forty), who was the sister of Ygnacio de Soto.

The following is Anza's 1775 list of soldiers (volunteers) and their families.

Vasquez, Juan	Family of six
Garcia, Antonio	Family of seven
Aceves, Antonio	Family of eight
Tapia, Felipe	Family of eleven
Gutierrez, Ygnacio	Family of five
Valenzuela, Agustine	Family of three
Alvarez, Luis	Family of four
de Soto, Ygnacio	**Family of four**

Pinto, Pablo	Family of six
Sotelo, Jose	Family of three
Bojorques, Pedro	Family of three
Pico, Santiago	Family of eight
Valencia, Jose	Family of five
Lopez, Sebastian	Family of five
Bernal, Juan	Family of nine
Sanchez, Jose	Family of five
Castro, Joaquin	Family of eleven
Felix, Vicente	Family of eight
Pacheco, Juan	Family of seven
Arellano, Manuel	Family of four

The following list includes the soldiers (full-time military) of the Presidio:

Moraga, Lieutentant Joaquin	Family of one
Grijalva, Sergeant Juan	Family of five
Bojorques, Ramon	Family of four
Gallegos, Carlos	Family of two
Amezquita, Juan	Family of eight
Alviso, Domingo	Family of six
Mesa, Valerio	Family of eight
Linares, Ygnacio	Family of six
Altamirano, Justo Roberto	Family of four
Peralta, Gabriel	Family of six

In October 1775, the Anza expedition left Tubac, Arizona. Tubac is often considered the official beginning of the expedition, although six hundred miles were already behind them and one thousand miles of deserts and mountains lay ahead. The expedition entered Alta California in January 1776. As soon as the group entered California, several of the men were immediately sent to San Diego to put down an Indian uprising. When the Indians saw the formidable array of soldiers, most opted for peace.

Despite the urgent situation at San Diego, the Anza colonists were able to move north towards Monterey and San Francisco Bay after a few weeks. The Presidio of San Francisco was officially founded on September 17, 1776. The mission of San Francisco de Asis, also known as Mission Dolores, was founded on October 9, 1776. In the early part of 1777, an agricultural colony had also been established at nearby San Jose. The Soto family stayed in San Francisco until 1785, when they moved south to San Jose.

Upon the colonists' arrival in San Francisco, more than one year had elapsed since they were first recruited for this expedition. All ties were now severed with New Spain. Life would drastically change for everyone. Gone were the dry deserts and the hot parched days. The climate along the coast was cool and moist. Winter rains nourished the rich soils, which produced abundant grass for livestock.

In the next five years perhaps three hundred more colonists would use the Anza trail, but this would be the last expedition of scale to enter California from New Spain. The new immigrants with their livestock would become the foundation for the future of this new land.

The Anza colonists had not only doubled the number of settlers in California but had also greatly increased the number of cattle and horses. The land route into California depended on the good will of the Indian population. Anza realized this and worked tirelessly to cultivate their friendship. However, later settlers became careless and in 1781 the Yumas attacked and killed the soldiers in a military garrison along the route to California. This would make Alta California once more a virtual island. For several years active colonization came to a close and after the 1780s only seaborne reinforcements were sent to California.

INTRODUCTION   21

Courtesy: Bill Strasen

1775/76 Anza Expedition Overland Route

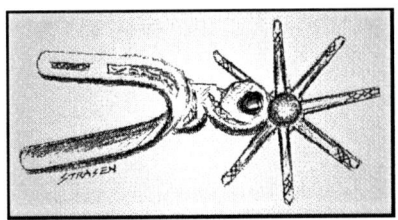

GENERATION 1 (YGNACIO)

Ygnacio Soto's existence in New Spain (Mexico) was one of dire poverty. While the Anza expedition provided the possibility of a new life, the concern Ygnacio must have felt for his family was considerable as they traveled through primitively charted territory, facing the uncertainty of hostile Indian attacks. A letter of November 17, 1774, from Anza to Viceroy Bucareli in Mexico City was quoted by Richard Pourade in *Anza Conquers The Desert* (1971):

> Complying with what your Excellency is pleased to order me with regard to the forty families who might go with me to occupy the river of San Francisco, let me say that the people whom I consider best suited for the purpose and most easy to get without causing a lack in their county, at the same time that the individuals sought may be benefited, are those of the alcaldias of Culiacan, Sinaloa and Fuerte, in the province of Sonora. Most of their inhabitants I have just seen submerged in the direst poverty and misery, and so I have no doubt they would most willingly and gladly embrace the advantages which your Excellency may design to offer them....

But the people recruited for New California were so poor that they had to be supplied with money and clothing. The men were to be soldiers only in a sense of being armed for any possible trouble. The harsh lands, outside of the few little valleys that could be irrigated without expensive works, and the dwindling mining, had left them with few possessions attractive enough to hold them on the edge of the empire. The New California of which they had heard, from the reports of those who had gone with Portola and Serra, and from Anza himself, was a land of sunshine and plenty.

The planning required for this expedition was extensive. Due to the severe terrain, everything had to be loaded and packed by horseback and mules; there were no wagons on this trip. This also meant that every morning the horses and mules had to be loaded, only to be unloaded again in the evenings.

Only ten tents were available for thirty families—tents that also required setting up and dismantling each day. Imagine the cramped quarters inside them, the rain, the windstorms, and the cold weather as the people crossed the high deserts during the winter months. There could be no turning back. Deserters would be hunted down and whipped. However, Ygnacio knew this expedition would provide the rare opportunity to escape the poverty in New Spain.

The expedition was an extremely difficult journey. Crossing over the high desert in freezing temperatures during the frigid winter months, dealing with inadequate food supplies, little water, and the unknown, must have been daunting. The lack of drinking water was a huge obstacle for the large herd of animals. To better deal with this situation, Anza divided the herd into three groups. This was necessary to allow the highly limited and sparse water holes time to refill between the three groups of thirsty animals. In the winter of 1775-76, one of the coldest on record, many of the weakened animals perished in the snow and freezing temperatures. The colonists persevered and survived, however, due largely to Anza's leadership skills.

Ygnacio Soto was born in Mocorito, Sinaloa, in 1749 and was baptized on February 20, 1749. He died on February 23, 1807, in Santa Clara, California. In 1773 he married Maria Barbara Espinosa (1760-1797). They apparently had thirteen children from 1774 to 1794. Shortly after Maria Barbara died, Ygnacio married (1798) Maria Rosalia Vasquez (b. 1785). This second marriage produced one son, Eugenio Antonio Soto, born in 1805. Soon after Ygnacio's death, Maria Rosalia married again, in 1807.

Ygnacio Soto is mentioned in Charles Shinn's book *Pioneer Spanish Families in California* (1896). While listing many of the original families in early California, Shinn writes: "The first of the Sotos was Don Ignacio [Ygnacio], a pioneer of 1776." Many families (Castros, Picos, Avilas, Pachecos, Lugos, and the Sotos) are identified in this short book. Ygnacio became the Soto patriarch and founded the northern branch of this large family.

A hardship often overlooked was the vulnerability to the perils of pregnancy and childbirth. As identified in *Chicana Critical Issues* (1993), Norma Alarcon and her fellow authors state:

> Eight persons, or twenty-five percent, of the thirty-two married women journeying north were pregnant at the start of the journey. Of the eight pregnant women, five had miscarriages, and three gave birth to children who survived the journey.

Fortunately, Barbara (Espinosa) Soto was one of the three women who were able to withstand the rigors of this difficult excursion while carrying her third child, Francisco. Francisco Soto was the first non-Indian child born in San Francisco. Francisco's baptism was entered into the Mission Dolores records in Father Francisco Palou's own hand. Francisco carries #1 alongside his name in the Mission Dolores records and is buried at the Mission Dolores cemetery in San Francisco.

William Heath Davis, who was prominent in San Diego history, wrote in *Seventy-Five Years In California* (1929/1967):

> Across San Lorenzo Creek (near present-day San Leandro) was the Rancho San Lorenzo Bajo, owned by Francisco Soto, with one to two thousand cattle and three to four hundred horses.

Davis continues:

> To the south of Francisco Soto was the mission of San Jose, which had eight thousand head of cattle, about three thousand horses and eight to ten thousand sheep, and fifteen to eighteen hundred Christianized Indians, all under the charge of Don Jose Jesus Vallejo, the administrator of the mission.

In his *"California Pioneer Register and Index 1542-1848"* (1964), Hubert Howe Bancroft, the well-known historian, confirmed:

> Francisco Soto was the first child born at San Francisco in 1776, son of Ignacio [Ygnacio]. He became a soldier in S. F. comp. [San Francisco company], was a corp. [corporal] in 1810, and was promoted to sergt. [sergeant] for bravery in an Ind. [Indian] campaign of that year; also made an expedition in '13 [1813] and another in '20 [1820].

On August 13, 1795, Francisco married Ana Maria Antonia Higuera at Mission Santa Clara. This union would produce seven children from 1797 to 1810. Their children married into the Castro, Pacheco, and Briones families. *Californio Voices: The Oral Memoirs of Jose Maria Amador and Lorenzo Asisara* (2005), as recorded by Mora-Torres from stories by Jose Maria Amador and Lorenzo Asisara, mentioned Francisco Soto:

> In 1819, an expedition left San Francisco led by Captain Don Luis Antonio Arguello and composed of seventy-three soldiers, one officer, Second Lieutenant Sánchez, and Sergeant Francisco Soto. Among the soldiers were twenty-five infantrymen from the San Blas Company, yet every one of them was mounted.

This personal account of a military Californio portrays Francisco Soto as a rough and brutal man. It should be noted, however, that these were difficult times that hardened most men. Sergeant Francisco Soto was well-known in Alta California for his bravery and also for coming from an old-line family; because of this, he was considered a *sargento distinguido*.

Another story from Mora-Torres's book regarding Francisco Soto discusses Soto as being in charge of disbursing mission property from the abandoned Mission Santa Cruz (founded in 1791):

> Francisco Soto came afterwards to finish the rest. Even the roof tile was taken during his bouts of drunkenness. Afterwards, he wanted to treat Indians as during the mission days, with kicks and sticks.
> The Indians rebelled one afternoon when he [Francisco] was half drunk. They got him and made him understand that if he continued committing [his cruelties] he would not live very long. Then, he went to Monterey and brought Joaquín Soto, his brother, and Vicente Cantúa, his brother-in-law, to keep him company. Francisco Soto was a lieutenant or a second lieutenant in the militia. The time came when Soto arrested the Robles brothers (Nicolás, Abelino, Secundino, another one called El Chato) for some reason, which I do not recall, and he tried to put a rope around their necks as had been done with Indians. They resisted. Abelino was the bravest and the most disobedient of them. Soto was walking around somewhat drunk and had some soldaditos [little soldiers—a denigrating term] with him. In his drunkenness, he issued orders to the soldiers to discharge their weapons at Abelino. This one separated himself from his brothers and while resting himself on the wall he told them

that they had him and they could kill him but that he would not allow them to put a cord on his neck. The soldiers pointed [the weapons] at Albelino and they fired at him, mostly at the sides but one of the shots (fired by Pantaleón Higuera) hit Abelino in the groin area, from which injury he died two or three days later.

Because of this action, the widow of Abelino Robles disguised herself as a man, and carrying a dagger, awaited the chance to kill Francisco Soto. His friends and fellow soldiers convinced him to leave Santa Cruz so that he could escape the fury of the woman and of the father and brothers of the deceased person. During the night he crossed the swollen river and went to Monterey. He never came back again. For a few days longer Joaquín Soto and Vicente Cantúa remained there.

Afterward, José Antonio Bolcoff came to administer the property.

This personal account was signed by Lorenzo Asisara. As documented in this incident, the Indians of this period were treated harshly by many Californios.

Antonio Soto, son of Francisco and grandson of Ygnacio Soto, was born in 1797 at Mission Santa Clara. According to *The History of Alta California* (1996), translated by Rose Marie Beebe and Robert M. Senkewicz:

> All three generations of Soto men – Ignacio [Ygnacio], Francisco, and Antonio – served as soldiers at the San Francisco presidio. Antonio was killed in 1829, during the expedition against Estanislao.

Estanislao was an Indian leader who left Mission San Jose with all the members of his tribe. He escaped and fled to a fortified place and vowed he would rather die than be captured by the soldiers. Sergeant Don Antonio Soto and fifteen men were quickly outfitted and given the task of bringing this rogue tribe under control. However, it proved extremely difficult because Estanislao's tribe used the cover of dense willow trees, intertwined by a great number of shoots from climbing vines for their protection. Beebe and Senkewicz further report:

> Since this sergeant [Antonio Soto] was one of the old guard, he deserved the confidence of his superiors. He also had the advantage of knowing the language of those Indians; but he was too daring, and this fault worked to his disadvantage, resulting in disastrous consequences.

In a hasty move, Antonio Soto entered the thicket and was promptly shot with an arrow below his right eye. The arrow shaft was removed quickly, but the flint arrowhead remained embedded in his face. This wound proved fatal for Sergeant Soto, who died within a few days.

Estanislao proved difficult for the army to control as two later attempts with additional soldiers were necessary before he was captured— a very important milestone for the Spaniards because the Indians had to be controlled for success of the mission system.

All of Ygnacio's children born after 1785 were baptized at Mission Santa Clara, supporting the claim that the Soto family moved to the San Jose area. The San Jose-Santa Clara area had become an important farming region for Alta California. Also supporting this fact was the newsletter from Bartolome Sepulveda, Volume 8 Number 2, "*Noticias Para Los Californianos*" (March-April 1976) which stated:

> MONTEREY, JANUARY 4, 1794 – Cabo Gabriel Moraga is ordered to Monterey for a conference with Jose Arguello and Governor Jose Joaquin de Arrillaga, and leaves Ignacio [Ygnacio] Soto in charge of the Pueblo de San Jose.
> MONTEREY, JULY 5, 1794 – Jose Arguello requests that a shipment of grain, onions, garlic, and chickens be sent from the Pueblo de San Jose to Monterey by way of a pack train to be led by Ignacio [Ygnacio] Soto.

The children of Ygnacio Soto and Maria Barbara (Espinosa) Soto were:

1. Maria Antonia Francisca Soto   b. 1774   d. 1815
   m. 1787 Bartolome Ygnacio Pacheco
2. Jose Antonio Soto   b. 1775   d. 1818
   m. 1794 Juana Maria Amesquita
3. Francisco Jose de los Dolores Soto   b. 1776   d. 1835
   m. 1795 Ana Maria Higuera
4. Francisco Maria Soto   b. 1777   d. ?
   m. 1796 Maria Trinidad Hernandez
   m. 1831 Maria Antonia Butrino
5. Damasio Soto   b. 1778   d. 1827
   m. 1807 Maria Antonia Alviso
6. **Isidoro Soto**   **b. 1780**   **d. 1847**
   m. 1799 Maria Marcela Linares   b. 1777   d. ?

7. Maria Rafaela Soto   b. 1782   d. 1833
    m. 1795 Juan Mesa
    m. 1818 Francisco Maria Garcia
8. Maria Ana Josefa Soto   b. 1783   d. 1838
    m. 1796 Jose Antonio Sanchez
9. Jose Joaquin Soto   b. 1784   d. 1850
    m. 1803 Maria de la Luz Ines Berreyesa
    m. Maria Juana Lorenza Butron
10. Maria Bernarda Soto   b. 1785   d. 1842
    m. 1801 Jose Joaquin Higuera
11. Tomas Antonio Soto   b. 1786   d. 1821
    m. 1807 Maria Luisa Peralta
12. Juan Antonio Soto   b. 1787   d. ?
    m. 1809 Maria Petra Pacheco
13. Rafael Soto   b. 1789   d. 1839
    m. 1811 Maria Teresa Boronda
    m. 1819 Maria Antonia Mesa
14. Maria Fernandia Soto   b. 1790   d. 1826
    m. 1805 Damaso Antonio Rodriguez
15. Juan Soto   b. 1794   d. 1794

Ygnacio's second marriage was to
    Maria Rosalia Vasquez   b. 1785   d. ?
    (Daughter of Tiburcio Vasquez and Maria Ana Antonio Bojorquez)
16. Eugenio Antonio Soto   b. 1805   d.1838-39
    Maria Rosalia Vasquez's second marriage was to Jose de la Luz Garcia in 1807, died in 1835.
The third marriage of Maria Rosalia was to Jose de la Luz Robles in 1835 at Mission Santa Cruz.

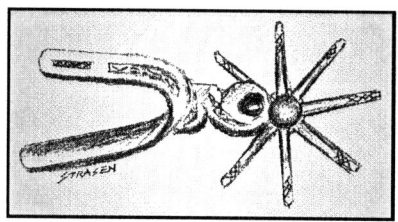

GENERATION 2 (ISIDORO)

Isidoro Soto was the sixth-born of Ygnacio's many children. He was born in San Francisco on February 5, 1780. Bancroft's *"California Pioneer Register and Index 1542-1848"* mentions him:

> [Isidoro], soldier retired with rank of lieut [lieutenant] '44, in '36 at Mont. [Monterey], age 55, wife Marcel Linares; married sons Lazaro and Joaquin.

Isidoro married Maria Marcela Linares in 1799. Marcela, born in 1777, was the daughter of Ygnacio Antonio Linares (a soldier of the Presidio of San Francisco) and Gertrudis Rivas. This marriage produced only two children, somewhat unusual for the time since families tended to be large. As quoted in Beebe and Senkewicz's book *Testimonios: Early California Through the Eyes of Women, 1815 – 1848* (2006), Dorotea Valdez's interview discusses how large the early families in California were:

> I must not forget to mention that during the early days of this country, in fact before the arrival of the Americans, our population increased very rapidly. It was not unusual to see a mother leading twenty-four children to church. And all these children had the same father. I am not exaggerating when I state that the average number of children raised by one mother was usually more than eleven and not less. However, ever since the Americans took possession of this country, sterility has become very common. The American women are, very fond of visiting doctors and swallowing medicine. This is a sin that God does not forgive.

The large family numbers in early Alta California were corroborated in Jo Mora's book *Californios* (1949):

> The average California family ran to a dozen children, more or less. But this was only the insignificant average. J.A. Castro counted twenty-six. When one Juan Cota died, he left five hundred living descendants. One Californian was the father of thirty-six children, twenty by his first marriage, sixteen by his second.

Jo Mora further elaborated on how everything grew in California; even cattle and horses multiplied at a tremendous rate due to the favorable climate and growing conditions. This may have been the reason that many of the pioneers became vaqueros. It was a necessary occupation because of the large numbers of livestock, which grazed over the open countryside. However, not all of the pioneers made a living as colorful vaqueros; some resorted to living a violent life of lawlessness.

Very little information is available on the life of Isidoro Soto. To better understand life during this time, information regarding current events of the time will be discussed here.

As population and tensions grew in dealing with Anglos in Alta California, many Californios were forced into a life of crime. In Reinstedt's *Ghosts, Bandits and Legends of Old Monterey* (1972), a great deal was written about Tiburcio Vasquez, the most infamous bandit around Monterey. Vasquez was often compared to Joaquin Murrieta, one of California's most well-known outlaws. Tiburcio was born in Monterey in 1835, and as Reinstedt explains about his fellow bandits:

> They were admired and feared by even those who knew them, and they were protected and sheltered by these very same people. They chose similar areas in which to hide out after their escapades (primarily the Cantua Canyon area of San Benito County). Their side-kicks and running mates were considered to be among the most heartless and cruel men in the state. Manuel Garcia, alias Three-fingered Jack (said to have hung six Chinese up by their hair and slit their throats for the fun of watching them die), being Murieta's [*sic*] companion and bodyguard, while Juan Soto, alias the Human Wildcat (labeled "the fiercest outlaw in California," was said to be bloody and ruthless [so that] "even his own companions feared him") was, for a time, Vasquez's partner in crime.

As previously mentioned, mission records show Ygnacio Soto as having married twice. His second wife was Maria Rosalia Vasquez, who was the daughter of Jose Tiburcio Vasquez and Maria Antonia Bojorquez. Ygnacio was thirty-six years older than Maria Rosalia. Jose Tiburcio Vasquez was the grandfather of the Monterey outlaw Tiburcio Vasquez (same name), who was hanged in San Jose in 1875. The connection between the Soto family and Vasquez family was close in that Ygnacio married into the Vasquez family as a second marriage and, later, Jesus Soto (son of Francisco, grandson of Ygnacio Soto) married the sister of the outlaw Tiburcio Vasquez. The Soto's historic adobe at 460 Pierce Street in downtown Monterey was next to the Vasquez family adobe in that same city.

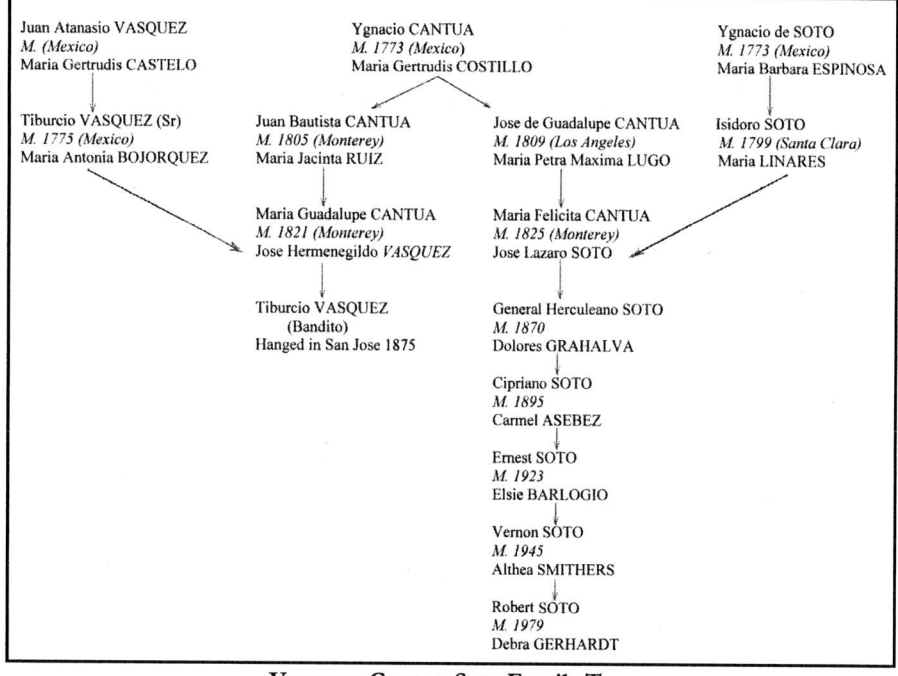

Vasquez-Cantua-Soto Family Tree

To better understand Tiburcio Vasquez and why he pursued the life of a bandit, we must consider the times. Tiburcio's grandfather Jose Tiburcio Vasquez, with his wife and four children, was part of the 1775 Juan Bautista de Anza expedition. In 1802 Jose Vasquez helped found the new settlement of San Jose and became its first mayor. In 1841 the overland migration of Yankee settlers into Alta California began with the Bartleson-Bidwell party. This major event, as well as the discovery of gold in 1848 in the Sierras, opened the floodgates for "Yankee" immigration into Alta

California. Then in 1850, the California Foreign Miners Tax severely penalized anyone but the Anglo natural-born U.S. citizens. This law effectively eliminated the Californios from mining for the precious gold nuggets, even though they had taught the Yankees the trade. The native-born, or old-line Californios, believed they were being shoved aside in their beloved homeland. Then on August 11, 1835, young (outlaw) Tiburcio Vasquez was born in Monterey and was witness to all these changes.

In 1836, Mexicans and Texans began fighting but the Mexican-American War of 1846 officially began with Texans declaring their independence against the Mexican government. Texas became an independent republic for nine years under the Lone Star flag. In 1842, (when Tiburcio Vasquez was just seven years old), Commodore Thomas ap Catesby Jones raised the flag of the United States at Monterey. Later Commodore Jones realized his premature error and apologized to the California governor. In 1846, the early American military pioneer John C. Fremont openly supported Yankee settlers and seized Colonel Mariano Vallejo and other important Californios, who were jailed and harshly treated for a two-month period.

According to Jose Antonio Burciaga's *Drink Cultura: Chicanismo* (1993), California Governor Pio Pico stated at this time:

> We find ourselves threatened by hordes of Yankee immigrants who have already begun to flock into our country and whose progress we cannot arrest.

Americans strongly believed in "Manifest Destiny," which they felt gave them the sacred right to expand their territory from the Atlantic Ocean to the Pacific. Partly due to this belief, war eventually erupted between the United States and Mexico in 1846. Two years later, in 1848, the war ended with the signing of the Treaty of Guadalupe Hidalgo. Overnight, thousands of "Mexicanos" became citizens of a foreign government. The breaking point came with the discovery of gold in 1848, with Yankee settlers overrunning California. The young Tiburcio Vasquez witnessed all these changes to his native California, changes that did not set well with him. The Vasquez family, once proud citizens of New Spain (Mexico) had been considered distinguished. Now the native-born Californios became second-class citizens in their own land.

Lynching of "greasers" became so common during the 1840s and 1850s that newspapers didn't even bother to report them. Leonard Pitt in *The Decline of the Californios* (1966), states:

"Greasers" had public opinion ranged against them from the outset: "To shoot these Greasers ain't the best way," one lyncher is quoted as saying. "Give'em a fair jury trial, and rope'em up with all the majesty of the law. That's the cure."

These were the times in which Tiburcio Vasquez was raised. Professor Rodolfo Acuña, author of *Occupied America: A History of Chicanos* (2004), wrote:

> Resistance also manifested itself in anti-social behavior. When the colonized cannot earn a living within the system, or when they are degraded, they strike out. The most physical way is to rebel.

According to information in Burciaga's *Drink Cultura: Chicanismo*, the editor of *The Los Angeles Star*, Major Benjamin Truman, interviewed Vasquez and revealed the following perspective on his life of crime:

> My career grew out of the circumstances by which I was surrounded. As I grew into manhood I was in the habit of attending balls and parties given by the native Californians, into which the Americans, then beginning to become numerous, would force themselves and shove the native born men aside, monopolizing the dance and the women. This was about 1852. A spirit of hatred and revenge took possession of me. I had numerous fights in defense of what I believed to be my rights and those of my countrymen. The officers were continually in pursuit of me. I believed we were unjustly and wrongfully deprived of the social rights that belonged to us. So perpetually was I involved in these difficulties that at length I determined to leave the thickly settled portions of the country, and did so.

Burciaga describes the first encounter between Vasquez and the law, which occurred at a dance. A fight broke out between three Californios (including Tiburcio) and several Yankee men. The native-born men considered the Yankees to be aggressive and rude to the Californio women. A law officer came to settle the fight, the lights went out, and a man was found lying dead on the floor. Two of the native men were caught and hanged after a short trial. Tiburcio Vasquez managed to escape, but this incident began his life of crime.

The law at this time was Anglo-American law, not favorable or familiar to the native-born. Tiburcio had little choice but to run and live outside these repressive conditions. He fled to his family and asked his mother "for and obtained her blessing and at once commenced the career of a robber."

Joaquin "Jack" Soto, who started Soto's Market in Cambria in 1917, recalled in an oral-history interview by his daughters, hearing old family stories of the Vasquez gang visiting the Adelaida "Dry Bones" Soto family ranch. Dry Bones was the name given to the later Soto family homestead in Adelaida. The name was derived from the bleached white bones of cattle that littered the ground after the great drought of 1862-64. Jack Soto reminisced from his childhood memories:

> It was a group of men that came and would spend the night on some place on their ranch because it was all very hush-hush. They never stayed any length of time. They would come maybe tonight and leave the next morning. As he [Jack] said they thought in later years that they were this bandit group. They never discussed it or talked about it but they knew that these men were on the ranch.

The Vasquez family appeared to rely on the friendship of the Soto family during this time of turmoil.

In Angus MacLean's book *Legends of the California Bandidos* (1977), it's evident that Vasquez spent a great deal of time around the Central Coast.

> In that first half-century following his hanging [in 1875], Vasquez remained very much alive in the memories of old-time residents of Central California; for this was Vasquez country, and the exploits of El Bandido Bravo were still the subjects of fireside tales.

MacLean further comments:

> In the three and a half years following Vasquez' release from San Quentin in August of 1863, his closest compadres were 'the human wildcat' Juan Soto and the gentleman Thomas Redendo, alias Procopio, alias Tomas Murrieta, said to have been a nephew of Joaquin Murrieta.

The relationship of my family to Juan Soto is unknown, but because his flamboyant and colorful personality continues to prove interesting, his story is worth noting here. A reprint on June 3, 1934, *San Francisco Chronicle* of an article titled "Juan Soto" (originally published on May 15, 1874) reads as follows:

> Juan Soto, [was] a desperado less known than Murietta [sic], but a companion to Murietta [sic]. He was half Indian and half Mexican and of very low character. Soto operated around the Livermore Valley on down to Monterey. He was able to escape capture for many years but was tracked down by Sheriff Morse in January, 1871. Soto's band had raided a small store and murdered the shop-keeper. In this way Morse was able to get on his trail and in the middle of January Soto was killed. Thus ending the terror of the early California desperadoes.

Unlike living as an outlaw, ownership of property was considered the accepted way to achieve success for most prominent citizens. To become a Spanish "Don" carried special prestige for the Californio. Frances Conley discusses Rancho life in Alta California. In the *Long Road to Rancho San Pablo* (which is exclusively devoted to the early day Castro family), Conley states:

> In 1823 the house, which had been built by the mission Indians almost ten years earlier, was ready for them. It was a long narrow house of adobe bricks, with three rooms and a parlor, laid out in a row, each room giving entrance to the next. The roof was thatched, and the floor was of bare earth. Since cooking in California took place out of doors or in a separate outside shelter, the only interior heat was supplied by an open pan of charcoal on the floor. The house must have been cold nearly all the time in the cool San Francisco climate; and it was a dark house even in the daytime, with only light coming through a few windows in the three-foot-thick adobe walls.
>
> Furniture was sparse, and most of it was very rough, though there may have been a few manufactured pieces brought by trading ships from Boston. Beds were sturdy frames with rawhide strips laced beneath a pad which served as a mattress. But the coverings very likely were of lovely embroidered work done by the women of the family. In the small and crowded house, unmarried men and boys simply threw down their blankets on the covered corridor around the house, or in the garret under the roof.
>
> Food was plentiful but unsophisticated: tough beef, beans, onion, wheat and corn, peppers, eggs, poultry, and local wines, with fresh fruit in season.
>
> Always there were Indian servants to do the housework, but Spanish women spent endless hours creating their beautiful embroidery and lace,

and there could have been little time left unfilled, with all the duties of family life and the women's unending preoccupation with religious observances.

The men worked hard, though it is often said that they would do no work which could not be done from the saddle.

The Soto family married into the prominent Castro family on at least two occasions. Francisco and Gabriela Castro had a daughter (baptized at Mission Dolores) named Maria del Carmen, who married Joaquin Soto (brother of Isidoro Soto) in 1822. In 1823, Francisco and Gabriela Castro's oldest son, Pablo Antonio Maria Castro, married Maria Barbara Rufina Soto (daughter of Francisco Jose Soto and Ana Maria Antonia Higuera).

By 1846, near the end of Mexican control over California, the Castro family owned all of western Contra Costa County, from the hilltops to San Francisco Bay. These vast holdings included Kensington, El Sobrante, Richmond, San Pablo, and El Cerrito. Then in 1851, the United States Land Commission was formed. The purpose of this governmental body was to review the validity of Mexican and other land-grant claims. According to Leonard Pitt in *The Decline of the Californios*:

> The board's [the Land Commission] function was to weed out the valid titles as defined by Spanish and Mexican law, the provisions of the Treaty of Guadalupe Hidalgo, the principles of equity, and the precedents of the United States Supreme Court.

Unfortunately for many of the Californios, all claims were considered invalid until they could be proven in an Anglo court of law. Between 1852 and 1856, a total of 813 cases came before the Land Commission, with 604 being confirmed. Wallace Ohles in *The Lands of Mission San Miguel* (1997) states:

> Some of the cases dragged on in the courts for several decades, and the average length of time required to secure evidence of ownership was 17 years from the time of submitting a claim to the board. It is no wonder that many Californios lost their land during the process.

Like most of the Spanish Dons, the Castro family's and the Soto family's beloved land-grant properties would be lost to mortgage holders, lawyers, and land speculators. (The Sotos' holdings, such as Cañada de la Segunda, will be detailed in the next two chapters.)

GENERATION 2   37

Another interesting account in Beebe and Senkewicz's *History of Alta California* describes the connection between the Osio family and the Soto family. Antonio Maria Osio's second wife was Narcisa Florencia Soto. This marriage took place at Mission Santa Clara on February 15, 1838:

> Narcisa was descended from two old military families in Alta California. Her paternal grandfather, Francisco Jose Dolores Soto [Ygnacio Soto's son], and her maternal grandmother, Juana Maria Lorenza Sanchez, were the first two children baptized at Mission San Francisco in 1776. By 1845 she had borne five children: Jose Antonio (1839), Juan de la Cruz (1840), Antonio (1842), Beatriz (1843), and Jose Manuel (1845).

This intriguing book discusses how Osio benefited from Governor Juan Alvarado's generous land-grant policy by receiving the entire Angel Island parcel on June 11, 1839. Three years later Osio also received Rancho Punta de los Reyes, on the coastline north of San Francisco. Then in 1844, Manuel Micheltorena (the new Governor of California) granted Osio the Rancho Aguas Frias, about 150 miles north of San Francisco.

In June 1846, Osio was apparently at Point Reyes when the Bear Flag Revolt began. Osio was warned to stay clear of the Sonoma area for his personal safety. The war between the United States and Mexico resulted in the U.S. Navy taking possession of Angel Island for strategic purposes. Beebe and Senkewicz reported:

> They commenced killing the cattle for military and naval uses and continued to do so until there were none left.

Osio, concerned for his life, fled Alta California and moved his family to Honolulu. He did not return to California until 1849, when he moved to Santa Clara.

The children of Isidoro and Maria (Linares) Soto were:

1. **Lazaro Soto**   b. 1801   d. 1851(?)
   m. 1825 Maria Felicita Cantua   b. 1809   d. ?
2. Joaquin Soto   b. 1803   d. 1852
   m. 1822 Maria del Carmen Castro   b. 1806   d. 1873

APPENDIX I

Encounter between Miller and Vasquez

An article by Rodney Johnson in the *San Luis Obispo Telegram-Tribune* of May 8, 1956, reads as follows:

Famed Encounter between Miller and Vasquez Took Place in Local Barroom.
An anecdote concerning 'debt of honor' between a cattle king and a robber baron in the early 1870s features an encounter between the two in the barroom of a San Luis Obispo hotel.

Henry Miller, the famous early day California cattle king who boasted at one time that he owned an acre of land for every one of his million head of cattle, always paid his debts.

When Miller, a German immigrant, was acquiring work renown in the early 70s, another immigrant was achieving fame in a far different manner.

He was Tiburcio Vasquez, who had taken up where his countryman, Joaquin Murietta, had been forced to leave off 20 years before.

It was inevitable that Miller and Vasquez should meet. One day as Miller jogged down the south slope of the Pacheco pass into the San Joaquin valley, he rounded a turn and there were four masked bandits. Miller handed over his well filled purse without a change of expression but he had a long way to go and it might prove embarrassing without funds. He said so.

The gang leader extracted two gold pieces from the cattleman's purse and tossed them to him.

'Pay me back the next time you see me,' he quipped.

Three months later, sitting in the lobby of a San Luis Obispo hotel, Miller heard a voice he remembered. It came from an adjoining barroom. He walked in and there was Tiburcio Vasquez.

Miller strode over to him, handed him $20 and said with a smile:
'Here's that money I owe you. Thanks very much for the use of it.'

And, the story goes, Tiburcio Vasquez that very night passed the word to the members of his gang that he, personally would shoot any one who even so much as looked at anything belonging to Henry Miller—the man who always paid his debts.

APPENDIX II

"1819 – A Bear Hunt"

To understand how difficult life was during this time a short story has been added here about a bear hunt as told by Juan Bautista Alvarado, who became governor of Alta California. This account took place in 1819 around the San Juan Bautista area and is included in this book since it would also be typical for the Soto family lifestyle. Thanks to publisher Heyday Books for permission to reprint this story from *Lands of Promise and Despair* (2001), by Rose Marie Beebe and Robert M. Senkewicz.

> My stepfather was a famous hunter and had good friends in the countryside, and for this reason he had two good shotguns of the kind that were then in use. Don Ignacio Ortega, one of the ranchers who lived near mission San Juan Bautista, invited him to come to his ranch for some time to hunt bears, which were very abundant and which were doing a great deal of damage to his livestock; and he offered him food and lodging for his family. My stepfather considered this to be a very profitable deal; and when he consulted my mother and me, it was jointly decided to accept Don Ignacio's invitation, on the condition that the skins of the bears would belong to us and that Don Ignacio would supply the old mares that were needed as bait for those beasts. These conditions were accepted by the rancher, we immediately sent some oxcarts to take us to his ranch. With this help we undertook the trip, carrying along our household furniture, which we had salvaged in the stampede from Monterey caused by commander [Hipolito—the privateer of 1818] Bouchard.
>
> As for me, I was delighted to become an apprentice rancher, because up to then I did not know how to ride a horse or do farm work; and bear hunting also appealed to me, since the skins were sold for six to ten pesos each, depending on their quality, to the captains of the ships that brought the annual accounts. They took them to the coast of Mexico, where they sold them at a great profit because they were used to decorate saddles and riding chaps, for which the Mexicans prepared them so as to make them very black and very pliable.
>
> We reached Don Ignacio Ortega's ranch, which was called San Ysidro. This old man had a family, horses, and much other livestock, and he gave us lodging suitable for bear hunters...

On the days when the rain did not keep him at home, my stepfather used to scout the countryside to choose the best hunting posts, so that the hunt could begin as soon as the worst of the winter was over. He had a very trustworthy horse that he called Coyote and that he always took on all his hunting expeditions. It was so used to gunfire that he could shoot over any part of its body without its making the slightest movement. He always kept it in the house and was concerned about its fodder and water that he would not eat until Coyote had eaten. He gave it sugar candy, tortillas, and other food from the kitchen; and so this animal always stayed close to the house, and if it did wander, it would only be a little way. My stepfather began by having me mount Coyote, and then he took one of the ranch horses and told me that he would lead me to the place where he was to begin the hunt.

We reached the edge of a wood, about a league from our house, where there stood a sturdy live oak all by itself; and my stepfather told me, 'This is the starting point for our operations. I have already made a wattle, or platform of woven twigs and branches, in this tree. When I decide on the right days, you will come for me again, because the bears usually come out of their lairs at nightfall, so that there is no point in waiting for them once it gets very late. The wattle has been set on two branches of the tree, and the palisade has been firmly lashed on. I will have to spend whatever time is necessary on the platform with my two guns, and the bait for the bears has to be down below. That way I shoot from very close to the animal, so that my shots hit right by the foreleg and enter the heart. Just the same, when you come to take me home, do not come up close to the tree. You will whistle to me from a distance, and I will answer you; and only if I do can you come as close as you like.'

All these instructions, together with those he gave me at home, taught me what I had to do in this bearish enterprise. We returned home very late, and my mother asked me what I thought of the bear business; and I told her that I already had all my instructions and that I was determined to go ahead with it, since this business was lucrative and was going to make some money for us to take back to Monterey.

Early in February we began our hunting operations; and so my stepfather spent the day cleaning his guns and preparing the ammunition, and I saw to it that Coyote was well saddled and fed. Don Ignacio had a mare taken out and killed, according to my stepfather's instruction, beneath the platform in the tree. Everything was well prepared. We set out at sundown, with my stepfather in the saddle and me behind him; and he told me once again, as he had before, how I was to come for him at midnight, and how, before coming up to the tree, I was to whistle according to his instructions and then wait for his reply. My stepfather climbed up to his platform, which I would say was no more than eight feet above the ground; and I went home to return at the time agreed on. He had chosen the second quarter of the moon so that I could have good light in which to get used to night riding.

Although at my age it was difficult to undertake so unaccustomed a chore, I got up at midnight to fetch my stepfather, because I was anxious to know the results of the first night's hunting; and so I started off on Coyote at a full gallop. Before reaching the tree I whistled as agreed, and he answered me; and hearing that, I pushed on as much as I could, because the horse balked at going up to the tree, as if something were holding it back.

My stepfather climbed down and came straight toward me, and I asked him, 'How is our business doing?'

He answered me, 'Just fine. I have killed three very big bears, the kind that do so much damage attacking Don Ignacio's cattle. Let's go now, and we will come back tomorrow to skin them.'

The next day we took our knives and went to skin the bears. Don Ignacio went with us and was greatly pleased with the success of the first night's hunt, because he could tell that the dead bears were some of the old ones that hunted down and destroyed his cattle. My stepfather told me that the skinning had to be done without detaching the claws from the hides, because this increased the value of the skins when the Mexicans made their chaps, letting the natural claws of the bearskin hang down from the bottom part of those chaps. Once we had stripped the bears, we laid the skins on a sledge of green boughs; and with Coyote pulling the sled, we took them to our house. Then we immediately washed them very well with water in order to get rid of all the ticks and other creatures that might be on them, and stretched them on a square wooden frame to keep them good and clean.

My stepfather told Don Ignacio that on that night he would not go to the platform but would let the bears come and eat the whole mare without the least interference, so that they would grow confident (this he called baiting the bears); but that the next day he should put out another mare in order to continue the hunt. In the course of the month of February, and following the strategy, my stepfather killed twenty-five bears in that first place and when he saw that he had to find another location because the bears were not coming any more, he chose a new spot some two miles from the ranch houses. I was delighted with the building of this second platform because it was closer to home, and so my nocturnal voyages would be shorter; but at any rate, patience was the word if I were to keep making money, and so I decided to work harder and more diligently.

In this second hunting post I proposed to my stepfather that I go with him to the blind to see how he killed the bears; and he answered me, 'You will have to be very calm and brave to do that, because you have no idea what it is like in these places the first time you do it. Bears are very cautious, and they have a very sharp sense of smell and hearing, and they observe everything very carefully before coming up to the bait. When the bear draws near, you have to keep absolutely still, because at the slightest suspicion of danger he will run off and not come back, even if that means going hungry.'

After telling me these things and giving me due warning, my stepfather agreed to take me with him to the blind; and we climbed up into the tree, asking Julian Cantua to bring Coyote at midnight to take us home. I had along a blanket which my mother had given me to wrap myself in, because it was very cold.

After night had fallen, my stepfather said to me, 'There comes a bear.' As I said before this platform, like the earlier one, was probably no more than eight feet above the dead mare; and looking at the way it was made, I thought the bear could smash it with one blow of his paw. This thought was very vivid in me as I saw that beast draw near the tree, and right away my whole body began to shake with an uncontrollable fear.

My stepfather touched me with his hand and in a very low voice told me, 'Keep still.' But I could not help it; panic had seized me, and my fear grew as the bear drew nearer; and as a result, the branches supporting our blind were moving in a way the bear could clearly hear, just as my stepfather had told me. The bear seemed to be coming up with a good deal of suspicion, because he stopped several times, which showed that he suspected danger in the place where the dead mare, the bait, was lying. The bear stopped some twenty paces from us because the leaves of the tree on which we were sitting kept moving with the trembling of my body. He moved in circles around the tree, and in my fear I came to believe that he was looking for a way to attack us on the tree and preparing to climb up the trunk on the oak. My stepfather did not for a moment stop watching these movements; and at last, the bear withdrew without coming to eat any of the bait, and my stepfather said to me, 'We have lost a fine skin.'

Very soon after this a female bear began to draw near us with two little cubs; and my stepfather told me, 'This female is going to replace what we have lost with the male. She is coming with her hungry cubs and will not pass up a chance to eat or take notice of any danger.' To be sure, as soon as the bear came close to the bait and the cubs smelled the dead mare, they moved ahead of their mother to start eating; and, either because she was as hungry as her cubs or because she saw that they met with no obstacle, she advanced to the spot with no caution whatsoever. At this point my stepfather got ready to shoot, in spite of the fact that I kept on trembling, though less violently than when the male bear had come. The shot was true, for it entered by the foreleg and hit the heart, instantly killing the bear. When they heard the noise of the gunfire, the cubs fled a short distance off; but seeing that their mother was not following them, they came back to the bait. Now I recovered my spirit; and once rid of the fears which had gripped me earlier, I said to my stepfather, 'Don't kill them; let's catch them alive and take them back to the house.' But he answered me, 'They are already too big and would defend themselves against us if we tried to do anything like that, and I could not be sure that they would not bite us and also scratch us with their claws – enough to lay us up in bed for a while. They have to be killed, so that when they are grown up they will not destroy Don Ignacio's livestock.'

And at that point he fired on one of the cubs and killed it. The third bear drew back a bit; but seeing that his mother and brother were not following him, he came back and kept on eating, while my stepfather reloaded his gun; and at the end, all three bears had been instantly killed. Just then Julian Cantua came with Coyote, and we went back to the house.

I told my mother the whole story of what had happened at the hunting blind, leaving out nothing; and she said, 'Now you know how to kill bears, you have satisfied your curiosity, and it would be better for us to pay Cantua to go at night for your stepfather. You have lost a lot of sleep and you are not used to this kind of work. I am afraid you will get sick. You had better help me with other things, without having to go after bears...'

My stepfather began to wonder what he might best do with the bearskins, since in Monterey he would have no place to keep them, and it would not be a good idea to leave them in the mission, either. While he was thinking about these things, there appeared a Spaniard, a merchant of sorts, one of those who came to this country and enjoyed the protection of their compatriots, the missionaries, and who carried on a trade, buying and selling things that might yield some profit. Taking advantage of the opportunity, my stepfather negotiated with that Spaniard, who could safely deposit the skins in the mission warehouses and wait to sell them at the right time to the officers who came on the ships with the King's accounts. My mother and he decided to sell the skins to the Spaniard for two hundred pesos, and thus they avoided having to take such a troublesome load to Monterey. The deal was made, and with this money we bought all that the family needed from the mission trading post.

Mariano Guadalupe Vallejo also writes a narrative regarding early California life in Frank Oppel's *Tales of Old California* (1989). This story elaborates on ranch and mission days in Alta California and tells of early rodeos, bull and bear fights, and also mentions the hunting of the early grizzlies:

> The governor of California appointed expert bear hunters in different parts of the country, who spent their time in destroying them, by pits, or shooting, or with the reata. Don Rafael Soto, [son of Ygnacio Soto], one of the most famous of these men, used to conceal himself in a pit, covered with heavy logs and leaves, with a quarter of freshly killed beef above. When the grizzly bear walked on the logs he was shot from beneath.

Grizzly bears have a long history in California of providing meat, clothing, and sport to the early explorers. These wild animals were considered extremely vicious and detrimental to agricultural enterprises. They were hunted fiercely, due in part to a bounty placed on their carcasses. The last grizzly bear in California was reportedly killed in 1922. Black bears and grizzlies were not known to co-exist, and it was not until the 1950s that the smaller black bear moved into the vacated Central Coast.

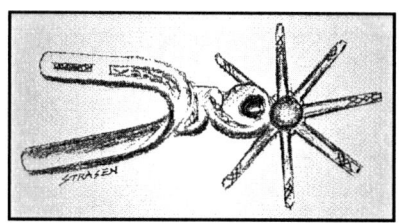

GENERATION 3 (LAZARO)

Lazaro, the elder son of Isidoro Soto, was born in December 1801 near Mission San Antonio, in Monterey County. Lazaro was baptized at the mission on December 17, 1801. In 1825, he married Maria Felicita Cantua (b. 1809), daughter of Jose Guadalupe Cantua and Petra Maxima Lugo. This would be a highly productive marriage, with eleven children being born. But many of them died early in life, typically due to disease and the many hardships they had to endure.

According to Bancroft's *"California Pioneer Register and Index 1542-1848"*:

> [Lazaro], son of Isidro, at Mont. [Monterey] '36 [1836], age 34, wife Solecita Cantera [Felicita Cantua], child. Isidro b. '28 [1828], General '31 [1831], Ramon '34 [1834], and Joaquin in '35 [1834]; grantee of Canada de la Segunda in '39 [1839]; at Mont. [Monterey] '46 [1846].

Although these dates and spellings do not exactly agree with the mission sources, they are extremely close and confirm the existence of the land grant of Rancho Cañada de la Segunda in Carmel.

From information discovered in files at Monterey's Colton Hall, it has been revealed that:

> The Rancho Cañada de la Segunda (second valley) was originally granted to Lazaro Soto in 1839. Consisting of 4,366.8 acres, the grant lay behind what is now Carmel-by-the-Sea Village, including the area known as the Mesa and the hills going towards the Mission San Carlos de Borromeo. In 1851

the United States government confirmed the grant which was then given to an Andrew Randall who bought the land for $500.

Lazaro is well documented for his kind treatment of the native Indians living on his land grants. The land passed through several hands until it became the property of Faxon Dean Atherton. Interestingly, in Generation 4 this same Atherton is also mentioned by Lazaro's son General Soto. By 1875 none of the five land grants in Carmel Valley were held by their original owners. Today, this property is prime real estate in one of California's most beautiful areas. File information also from Monterey's Colton Hall mentions the early-day builder Arthur Bowen. "Bowen came from nearby Sotoville, a settlement on Jose M. Soto's Rancho Santa Rita in Salinas, where he [Bowen] was born in January 1887."

Joaquin Soto, the younger son of Isidoro Soto (and brother of Lazaro), proved to be a fascinating individual who was often written about in Monterey history. Mayo Hayes O'Donnell wrote an article "Joaquin Soto's Will" on February 1, 1951, in the newspaper *Monterey Peninsula Herald*. The will was written in Spanish and is reported to be on file in the County Recorder's Office at Salinas. The will, translated in 1853, identified his possessions as an adobe home in Monterey and also Rancho El Piojo ("the louse"), which adjoined Mission San Antonio. This consisted of three square leagues (approximately 13,000 acres) of land, an adobe home with tile roof, two corrals, and a hundred head of cattle with five horses. Joaquin carefully listed all his possessions and all his debts. (The complete will appears in the appendixes to this chapter.)

According to information in Malcolm Margolin's *Preserving the Layers of History* (1997), four land grants were awarded on land presently occupied by Fort Hunter Liggett:

1. **Rancho San Miguelito de Trinidad**, some 20,000 acres lying along the Nacimiento River three leagues west of Mission San Antonio, had been established as a mission outpost as early as 1804.
2. **Rancho Los Ojitos ("Little Springs")**, some 9,000 acres, was established in 1818 by the mission for the pasturing of cattle. It occupied a narrow strip of land along the San Antonio River about three leagues south of the mission.
3. **Rancho Milpitas ("Little Fields")** encompassed the lands more or less surrounding the mission, its center being the area that is now the Fort

GENERATION 3   47

Hunter Liggett headquarters. In 1838 Ygnacio Pastor, an Indian who had been *alcalde* at the mission, was granted title to the rancho.

4. **Rancho El Piojo ("The Louse")** was a 13,000-acre tract southeast of Rancho San Miguelito. It was granted in 1842 to a soldier, Joaquin Soto, married to Maria del Carmen Castro and with many children.

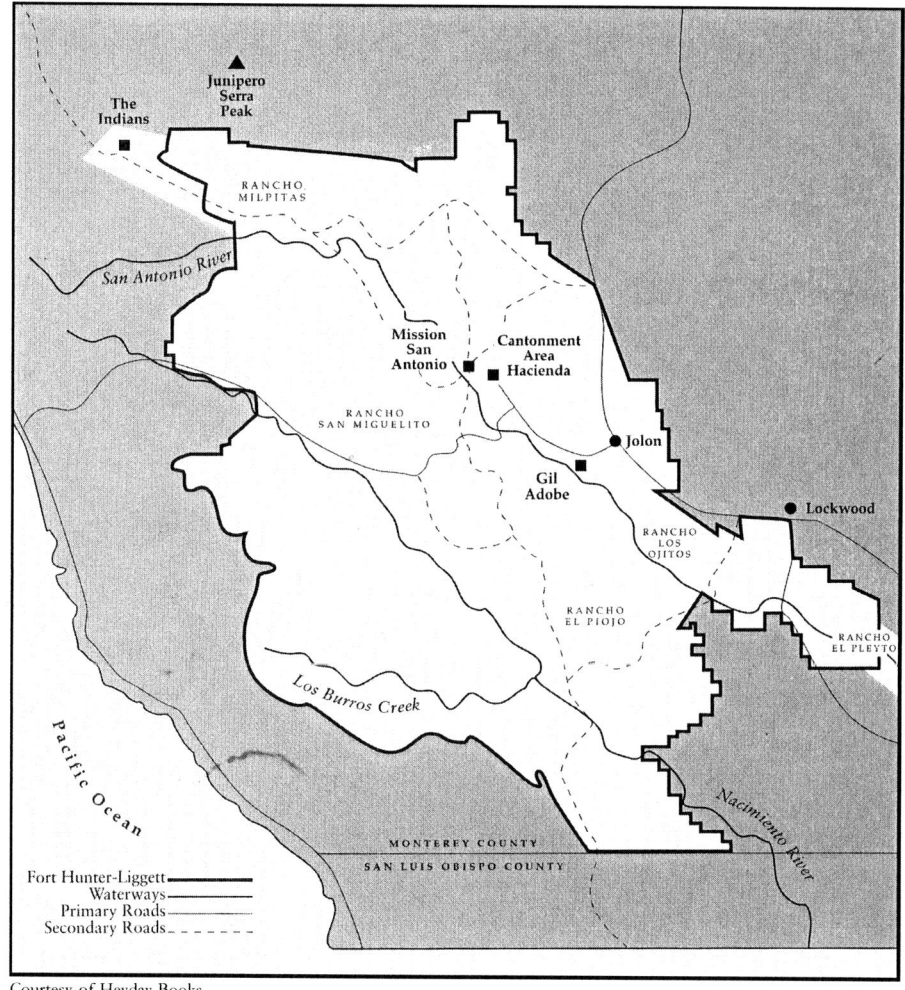

Courtesy of Heyday Books

Map of Joaquin Soto's Rancho El Piojo

Family researcher Newell Terrill discovered that Joaquin Soto was granted a second parcel in 1845. This land, consisting of 2,231 acres, known as Rancho Cañada de la Carpinteria (valley of the carpenter shop), was in the Prunedale area, north of Salinas. This grant was confirmed by Bancroft in his *Vol. 5, 1846–48, "Pioneer Register and Index 1840–45."*

However, it is unknown why this property was not identified and listed in Joaquin's will of 1852.

It's helpful to note that Miroslava Chavez-Garcia in her doctoral dissertation, "*Mexican Women and the American Conquest in Los Angeles* (1999)," discusses another Soto who held title to a Mexican land grant in the San Gabriel-Los Angeles area. Very few women held title to land in early California. Nearly all of them acquired their land through inheritance from their husband or father. However, there was a notable exception near San Gabriel:

> Casilda Soto, attained her land under circumstances that were less common among grantees. In 1844, she appealed to Governor Manuel Micheltorena for title to Rancho La Merced, property that originally belonged to San Gabriel (Los Angeles) Mission. She had lived there since 'some time ago', she explained, when ex-governor Juan Bautista Alvarado . . . had given consent and permission to do so. Morever, she added, she also deserved the land in exchange for the payments owed by the presidial military to (her deceased) husband. Micheltorena directed the Los Angeles alcalde to investigate Soto's eligibility for a grant. His response was straightforward and positive: Soto is an honorable widowed woman who has very good habits . . . has a house and livestock on the land. The priest at San Gabriel Mission, whom the governor also contacted for confirmation that the mission no longer occupied the land, endorsed Soto's request as well. But, Father Tomas Estenaga stipulated, though the property is vacant she has to pay fifty head of cattle to the mission in exchange for the concession. Soto agreed to the unusual terms, and Micheltorena awarded her title to the property. Only in rare circumstances, such as when a grant infringed on another's property, were grantees obligated to compensate the owner. Why the priest and the governor required her to pay for land that had been secularized and made part of the public domain remains unknown. Her willingness to cooperate, however, secured for her the property.

Maria Casilda Soto was born in April 1799 at Mission San Gabriel to Guillermo Soto and Juana Maria Perez Nieto. According to Marie Northrop's *Spanish–Mexican Families of Early California: 1769–1850*:

> Guillermo Soto was a soldier recruit of 1781; one of five single men in the contingent who arrived at San Gabriel on 14 July 1781 with Alferez Jose

Dario Arguello; at Santa Barbara in 1785; settled at Los Angeles in 1789; alcalde in 1798 and 1809.

The relationship between Guillermo and Ygnacio Soto is unknown. However, both men came from Sinaloa, New Spain (Mexico). As discussed by Wallace Ohles in *The Lands of Mission San Miguel*:

> In order to be considered as a possible grantee of land in California, it was required that the person be a citizen of Mexico, by birth or naturalization, and proclaim belief in the Roman Catholic faith. If the person were a naturalized citizen, he would need to be connected by marriage with a Mexican family.
> By 1846, 790 grants had been made in California to 725 individuals; only fourteen of these grants were made during the period of Spanish government. Land grants had to be occupied within one year; this requirement could be met by building a house and corrals, introducing livestock, or planting an orchard.

In 1848, California was annexed by the United States under the Treaty of Guadalupe Hidalgo (it would not become a state until 1850). Prior to 1848, a number of Mexican land grants were issued that turned the San Antonio Valley over to private hands. According to Malcolm Margolin in *Preserving the Layers of History*:

> In many aspects, the system of land grants resembled the Homestead Act of 1862 in which the U.S. government would offer its citizens free land in exchange for their residing on it and developing it. There were, however, differences, the most notable of which was in acreage. Whereas the Homestead Act, in theory at least, limited a person's allotment to 160 acres, it was not unusual for a Mexican land grant to encompass 10,000 acres and sometimes much more. After all, petitioners were relatively few, land in California was seemingly limitless, and ranching—the preferred occupation of most grantees—required much greater acreage than farming.

The descendants of Ygnacio Soto were grantees of many ranches in Alta California. The list includes the following ranchos: Cañada de la Segunda, El Piojo, San Matias, San Lorenzo, Cañada de la Carpinteria, Cañada Del Hambre, Capay, San Vicente, Los Vallecitos, and Bolsa Nueva.

Around 1846 in early California, many of the old-time Californios still did not recognize the legitimacy of the United States Government and had good reason not to trust it. After all, they were citizens of Mexico, once subjects of proud Spain, and California was founded and colonized by them. They were fearful of losing all the possessions they had worked so hard to acquire.

The children of Lazaro and Maria (Cantua) Soto were:

1. Monica Ascencion Soto	b. 1826	d. before 1836
2. Jose Isidoro (Lazaro) Soto	b. 1827	d. ?
m. 1849 Maria Rita Quiteria Arrieta		
3. Mariano Miguel Cipriano Soto	b. 1829	d. (at birth)
4. **General Herculeano Soto**	**b. 1830**	**d. 1906**
m. 1861 Maria Rosalia Quijada (?)	b. ?	d. 1866
m. 1870 Maria Dolores Grajalva	b. 1856	d. 1923
5. Guadalupe Epifanio Soto	b. 1832	d. 1832
6. Candido (Ramon) Soto	b. 1833	d. 1870
7. Manuel (Joaquin) Soto	b. 1835	d. 1917
8. Maria Josefa "Gertrudis" Soto	b. 1837	d. ?
9. Maria Eduviges Soto	b. 1840	d. before 1850
10. Maria Juliana Angela Amanda Soto	b. 1843	d. ?
11. Maria Longina Celestina Soto	b. 1845	d. 1850

APPENDIX III

Soto Monterey Adobes

Lara-Soto Adobe:

While visiting the historic center of old-town Monterey, I discovered that there are two separate Soto adobe homes in that city. One is the Lara Soto Adobe, at 460 Pierce Street, and the other is Casa de Joaquin Soto Adobe, at the corner of Carmelo and Cass streets.

The exact date that the Lara Soto Adobe was built is unknown, but some historians suggest 1842. Also, there appears to be conflicting information regarding the early owners of this property. One source in the Monterey Library Early California Room notes, "The adobe building was sold to Jesus Soto, and the assessment records of 1851 show the property assessed to him, reading one adobe back of Colton Hall." However, other historical records show that this property was deeded as a town lot to Dona Feliciana Lara on September 18, 1849. Reportedly, the original two-room adobe house was built by Francisco Soberanes and sold in 1851 to Jesus Soto. The front yard has a massive old cypress tree, said to have been planted over the grave of a child of one of the early occupants of this house. In turn, the adobe was occupied until the 1890s by Manuel Soto and his Native American wife, Felicida. Manuel, born in 1825 to Jose Ygnacio Soto and Maria de Jesus Lara y Zabala, was a well-known local woodcutter and barber. Felicida was a Gabrieleño Indian from southern California. In some accounts it has been speculated that, because of the similarity of names (Felicida and Feliciana), Feliciana was also the first deed-holder. Dona Feliciana Lara and Manuel may have been a blood relative of Jesus Soto. Manuel eventually sold the house to Antonio Dutra; however, it seems it was not his to sell. Dutra and his Native American wife, Ramona, lived on the property until it was determined that no one had paid the taxes for several decades. During this time, no one lived on the property and it was abandoned. It became a hangout for bandits, resulting in the adobe often being referred to as the "Bandit House." The house was sold in 1905 to pay back taxes.

To add more confusing information about this adobe, archivist-historian Dennis Copeland of Monterey stated:

True natives of Monterey were Mr. and Mrs. Manuel Soto who died here over 40 years ago. They lived in the old adobe which still stands on Pierce street, between Franklin and Jefferson streets. This rare photograph was loaned to The Herald by Capt. Herb Bispo of the Monterey Fire Department.

Monterey Peninsula Herald Photo

Over the years, the early ownership and occupants of Lara-Soto adobe have been misidentified. Jesus Soto never owned or lived in the building. Jesus Soto, the son of former soldier Francisco Maria Soto and Maria Trinidad Hernandez, lived with his family from the mid-1840s through the 1850s in a house adjacent to the Vasquez house and, probably, at some point lived in the Vasquez house with his family. He married Maria Concepcion Vasquez, sister of Tiburcio Vasquez (the infamous outlaw), in 1845.

In 1919, the property was purchased by Josephine Blanch, an artist and curator of the first local art gallery. Ms. Blanch restored and remodeled the structure in 1931 and again in 1940, using it as her residence for a while. In 1944 she sold the property to the famous writer John Steinbeck, who knew the house from his youth. According to John McCleary's pamphlet *Bandits, Ghosts and a Nobel Prize Winner Have Slept Here*, Steinbeck once wrote to a friend:

> It is a house I have wanted since I was a little kid, it is one of the oldest and nicest adobes in town—with a huge garden—two blocks from the main street and yet unpaved and no traffic…I've a wonderful sense of going home.

One can see from the fascinating history of the Soto pioneers, who counted outlaws and bandits amongst themselves, why they are an essential part of California's colorful history.

Joaquin Soto Adobe:

According to Planned Parenthood of Monterey County (which owns the Casa de Joaquin Soto adobe), Joaquin built one of the oldest adobes in 1823, currently preserved in Monterey. This home was built originally for his bride, Maria del Carmen (Castro) Soto. The Casa de Joaquin Soto adobe, built on land purchased from relatives, was home to four generations of Sotos spanning a hundred-year period. This modest home was lived in by the last family member, Augustine Soto, generally known in Monterey as "Count" Soto. As a young girl, Margaret "Dolly" Soto recalled visiting the Monterey adobes and Count Soto with her father, Joaquin "Jack" Soto of Cambria. Dolly's memories were of an eccentric member of the family.

This quaint little adobe sits on a beautiful hillside overlooking picturesque Monterey Bay. In its early days, the three-room rectangular building was gray and patched, with many unprotected bricks. Its adobe bricks were one-and-a-half-feet square and three-feet thick, bonded together with mud, broken tile, and twigs. The original thatched roof, common to early Monterey one-story houses, was later covered with tiles made by Indians who used forms made of various-sized tree trunks.

54   AN OLD CALIFORNIA FAMILY: THE SOTOS OF CAMBRIA

Courtesy: Monterey Peninsula Newspaper

The Historic Soto Adobe

An interesting story of Joaquin's family history pertains to his grandson Augustine "Count" Soto, who lived in the original family adobe in Monterey. Count refused to pay property taxes assessed against this property once owned by Joaquin. Count and his wife, with many children, lived in a small wooden house in front of the old adobe house facing Eldorado Street. The property became so messy, and the taxes due were so great, that the city finally evicted the family and pulled down the building on April 13, 1938. Count Soto was then, by his own admission, seventy-three years of age. He died four years later.

On July 9, 1948, *Monterey Bay News* ran a story by Nellie Imwalle Heneken recalling Augustine Count Soto's family recollections:

Fortunate is the person who knew well the late Augustine Soto; one of the most colorful characters of early Monterey and scion of a once wealthy and landed family; he could tell interesting tales with zest and a glint of mirth in his eyes.

One such tale as told by Count follows:

It seems that when Rev. Angelo Cassanova was the parish priest in Monterey in 1875, it was the custom of the people of his church to tithe themselves; taking a goodly portion of any good food which they happened to possess, to Father Angelo. These offerings usually took the form of a haunch of venison or a fat suckling pig; of the last Father Angelo was especially fond. He also favored turkey and fat chicken.

A relative of the Soto family, whom we will call Juan (although that was not his name) raised turkeys. Out of the flock of perhaps 30 turkeys which reached maturity under the skillful hands of his wife, Antonia, all would be sold but the two fattest and largest. These would as a matter of course, be taken to Father Angelo. They would be placed in the fenced yard for poultry, for the Father's regalement later.

One day, looking over the flock, Antonia spoke of the turkey's size and said they would soon be ready for market. She tied white strings on the legs of the two largest and fattest gobblers. Juan looked on. The two gobblers were unusually fat and large this year, it seemed to him. What a feast they would make for Father Angelo! Juan eyed them with disfavor.

'We sell our turkeys each year, all but the two fattest and biggest which we always give to Father Angelo. We never taste turkey. Yet, he has plenty of pork, chicken and turkey. It is sure as the neighbors say; we never have a fiesta in our home.'

'We have our health. We have always given the turkeys to Father Angelo, and we always will,' said Antonia with finality.

That year, when the turkeys were sold, the two fattest and largest birds had their legs tied together and were taken to the priest's house where they were placed in the poultry yard. When he placed the turkeys in the yard, Juan noticed that there were two fat roosters and two fat pigs there.

The next morning when Antonia went to throw out corn to their few hens, she stood in amazement and looked. There were two fat roosters and a fat pig in the yard. She called Juan, in great excitement.

'Juan! Come here quickly! It is a miracle! Last night I dreamed that I heard a pig grunting and squealing! We have been given this fat pig and two fat roosters!'

Juan came out slowly, yawning and rubbing his eyes.

'Yes, it is indeed a miracle,' he said 'I will butcher and cook them and we will have a fiesta. We will invite Father Angelo and all our friends,' and he hurried to bring wood for a fire.

So, the Father was invited to the feast and [so were] all the neighbors. When the food was cooked and the people began to come, Juan said happily to Antonia, 'It is indeed a good thing for a man to invite his friends to his home, and this miracle is intended to make it possible for us to treat our friends with the respect which they show us. Father Angelo shall sit at the head of the table,' and he carried chairs from a neighbor's house and set them around the table.

After the bountiful feast, the people sat around talking about the miracle which had come to Juan and Antonia. In time it became known to the people, that every year Juan and Antonia gave of their best to Father Angelo and every year was given to them, miraculously, food for a fiesta.

Could this story reveal a very clever Father Angelo who "seeded" this great feast and by doing so encouraged others to tithe the church? Or did Juan finally grow disgruntled with giving his fat turkeys to Father Angelo? Religion was very important in the lives of early-day Californios.

After the death of Count Soto, Mrs. Mary L. Greene, then curator of the Old Custom House in Monterey, bought the historic family adobe. But it took a year's search to clear the property title, which had been in litigation for a hundred years. Previously, this lengthy litigation blocked any attempts to purchase this highly valuable property. In 1958, Mary Greene left Monterey and sold the adobe to Dr. Scott Heath, who remodeled it and converted it into medical offices. In 1978, Planned Parenthood of Monterey County purchased the adobe.

Information gathered from a booklet written by the Monterey History and Art Association, of unknown authorship, was entitled *Casa de Soto:*

When Augustine [Count] de Soto passed quietly away one day in September of 1942 another segment of Monterey's colorful history slipped away also. He was as much a part of local history as anything to be found in the school books. He was one of the last links with the Spanish period in California.

APPENDIX IV

Don Rafael Soto

Being a large family, the Sotos settled in many areas of California. A remarkable article printed in *The Californians* magazine (date unknown) focused on the Soto family that settled in Palo Alto. There were four land grants given to old-time respected families in the 1830s in the area of Palo Alto. Most of early Palo Alto, carved from Rancho Rinconada del Arroyo de San Francisquito (little corner of the San Francisquito Creek), was granted to Rafael Soto. Rafael's father was Ygnacio Soto, and his brother was Francisco Soto, the first Spanish child to be born (1776) in San Francisco after the arrival of the Anza expedition.

From information in *The Californians* magazine:

Don Rafael Soto was 46 when his land was granted in 1835. Later there was the usual difficulty gaining U.S. title; Rafael's heirs received the official U.S. patent in 1872.

[Rafael] Soto settled on roughly 2,200 acres, part of the Corte Madera rancho along Alpine Road in about 1827 and, later, a portion of Mission Santa Clara's land after its secularization. It was in a bend in the creek and had been the headquarters of the mission's sheep ranch.

Not much is known today about Rafael and his wife Maria Antonia [Mesa]. According to Mission Santa Clara records, Rafael was born on April 17, 1789, the next to youngest of 13 children, and he married Maria Antonia in 1819 when she was 17. The couple had at least seven children plus two adopted orphans. Rafael's will, written 1839, lists nine and one yet unborn, so there probably were 10 children, all told.

In those days the creek [San Francisquito Creek in Palo Alto] was navigable by small boats to where Newell Road is today; here Rafael built a small wharf. Lumber was brought to the wharf over rough trails which eventually settled into Embarcadero Road, and supplies from San Francisco were deposited there.

The Sotos had a large house on Middlefield [Road] just north of Oregon Avenue. Almost no records chronicle their life there. In 1918 a Mrs. Juan Romero reminisced to historian Cora Older about attending balls at the Sotos. There is another report of a three-day party after Maria Luisa's 1839 wedding.

One record reports the Soto barn was moved to High Street where it became Paulsen stable, one of the first businesses of the fledgling town [Palo Alto].

Rafael Soto died in February 1839, just four years after acquiring his rancho. His widow Maria Antonia rode to Monterey to register the claim, and she was granted title to the land in 1841 by Governor Alvarado.

Thus Rafael did not live to see his daughter Maria Luisa marry a British naval officer named John Copinger (Coppinger) on February 23, 1839. Their wedding took place at Mission Santa Clara and was the first in the area involving an English-speaking person. Reportedly the bridal pair rode to the church on a single horse and returned to the Palo Alto rancho for a wonderful party that lasted three days and included the roasting of a whole steer.

John Copinger was the 1840 recipient of a San Mateo county grant, Rancho Cañada de Raimundo, where the newlyweds set up housekeeping. Copinger's exact arrival in California has been a mystery; it is known that he was with Jose Peña and Antonio Buelna in the 1836 Alvarado revolt, thus earning the governor's gratitude and his rancho of 12,545 acres.

The Copingers built an adobe, raised crops and cattle, built a dam and put up fences. Copinger became a justice of the peace for about half of present-day San Mateo County, allegedly closing his eyes to at least one still in his jurisdiction. (Making moonshine was against Mexican law too.) Just eight years to the day after their marriage, on February 23, 1847, John Copinger died at the age of 37, leaving Maria Luisa, age 30, with a large rancho and a child on the way. Maria Luisa returned to her mother's rancho and lived there quietly, until her life changed once again in January 1850.

Captain John Greer was an Irish Sea captain who, after sailing the world and learning Spanish in South America, arrived in San Francisco Bay aboard the Wild Duck in 1849. While men from his ship joined countless others rushing off in search of gold, he decided instead to board a small boat and explore the southern part of the bay.

By chance, he followed San Francisquito Creek inland and happened to meet the widow and heiress to two ranchos, Maria Luisa Soto Copinger, who lived nearby. He decided to stay on in the area, quite charmed by the land and its inhabitants. Greer rented land from Maria Luisa and started raising vegetables.

The two soon fell in love, married at the Santa Clara mission in 1850, and returned to the adobe at Rancho Cañada Raimundo to live. In a sentimental gesture, Maria Luisa brought with her to the rancho cuttings from Mission rose bushes, imported by the padres from Spain 75 years earlier. One, the pink Rose of Castile, was strongly fragrant and favored by the Spaniards for its special beauty. The roses thrived in their new setting, reminding Maria Luisa of her Spanish heritage as she entered an increasingly English-speaking world.

The Greers remained at Canada de Raimundo for about 15 years and had five children. In the early years of their residency they supposedly traded 1,000 or 1,200 acres of their rancho to a salesman named Dennis Martin (famous himself in San Mateo county history) for locks, latches, doorknobs and other such household hardware, probably worth about $10.

While the Greers were having trouble proving title to this rancho, Manuela Copinger, Maria Luisa's daughter, married, sold her share of the land to maintain a high lifestyle and built a large house at 3333 Woodside Road whose mortgage could not be maintained. Arguments over the rancho's borders lasted 80 years.

Meanwhile Cap'n John Greer became a leading citizen of Greersburg, now called Woodside. He became a justice of the peace and also was involved with schools and library. The Greers moved back to the Soto rancho [Rancho Rinconada del Arroyo de San Francisquito] in the 1860s and built a 22-room house on the northeast corner of Churchill and Alma.

In 1867, because of another of the constant land disputes of the era, the Greers decided to move the house onto property that was definitely theirs. This meant transporting it across the newly-built railroad tracks between the morning and evening trains, the only two there were. They cut a wide path through the dense chaparral on the site of the present Palo Alto High campus and, using horses to turn a giant winch, rolled the house on a site near the intersection of El Camino Real and Embarcadero, where it remained for nearly a century. [It was razed in 1952 to allow the building of the Town and Country Village Shopping Center.] Maria Luisa brought cuttings from the Rose of Castile and Canada de Raimundo to her new home in Palo Alto.

The house became a social center of the area. There were week-long parties with friends from San Francisco, and two cooks often prepared dinner for 25 guests. Their huge, Spanish-style barbecues were famous. In the evenings, the furniture would be pushed back, Cap'n John would recline in a comfortable chair at one end of the room, and the young people would dance.

One son of Cap'n John and Maria Luisa [Soto], Lucas Greer, survived well into the modern era. A shaggy-haired man in a black sombrero, he delighted in riding a white horse around the area. Even at

Courtesy: Palo Alto Historical Association
Soto-Greer House, El Camino Real and Embarcadero Street (Palo Alto); circa 1940

an advanced age, he sat tall in his saddle through long hours. He was often a central figure in parades and rodeos. Although he never married, he was reportedly a ladies' man who loved to dance and won trophies in waltzing contests. He sat on the porch of the tall, faded yellow house through his declining years into the 1940s, watching Stanford football fans walk by on Saturday afternoons.

Lucas recalled that in the Palo Alto of the late 1860s, there were six houses, thick underbrush everywhere except along the creek, horses costing $15 to $40, and land offered for $10 an acre. A French Canadian named Charley was thought to be a horse rustler. Lucas also remembered a vigilance committee that would hang horse rustlers if they caught them.

Sometime in the 1850s, John Greer had met the Seale brothers, Thomas and Henry, San Francisco contractors looking for pasture down the peninsula. One thing led to another, and the Seale brothers offered to try to secure title for the Soto heirs in exchange for half the rancho. Greer agreed, the brothers went to work on the case, and finally, years later, the patent was issued. The Soto heirs were declared the legal owners, and the Seale brothers were given 1,200–1,400 acres for services rendered. Thus, the Greers [Sotos] and the Seales were the largest landowners in what was to become Palo Alto.

No descendants of the original Rose of Castile bush [planted by Maria Luisa] taken from the Santa Clara mission in 1850 remain today.

GENERATION 3 · 61

APPENDIX V

The Last Will and Testament of Rafael Soto, 1839

*Translated from the original manuscript by F.M. Stanger, San Mateo Junior College, December 1937. The original was in the possession of Lucas Greer, grandson of the testator, and son of Maria Luisa Soto Greer. Rafael Soto would normally have signed his will with an X, before the witnesses; no such mark appears here, suggesting that the will could have been written a few days after his death, when the need for it became acute.

In the name of Almighty God, Three and One, and of the ever-virgin Mary our Lady, I, Rafael Soto, native and citizen of the pueblo of San Jose de Guadalupe in the Department of the Californias, legitimate son of Don Ignacio [Ygnacio] Soto and of Dona Maria Barbara Espinosa, both now dead, declare that, being in full and complete use of my judgment, I do execute my last will and testament in the following terms.

First: I commend my soul to its Creator and my body to the earth from which it was formed.

Item: I declare that I am married to Dona Maria Antonia Mesa, legitimate daughter of Don Jose Dolores Mesa and Dona Maria Josefa Villavicencio; that she came to me without dowry, and I have not given her any dowry or gifts; and that in this marriage I have had the following children: Maria Luisa Gonzaga, Juan Capistrano, Maria de Jesus, Maria Francisca Cecilia, Maria Dolores, Juan Crisostomo, Francisco de las Llagas, Jose Guadalupe, Estevan and one still unborn a quien dejo encomendado mi entierro y sufragios [to whom I leave my burial and suffrages].

Item: I declare that the following persons are indebted to me:

Don Estevan Yguera, five pesos in silver.

Don Cruz Chavoya, five pesos, four that I paid to Julian Cantua in wheat, and one for the tongue of a cart that he broke.

Don Felipe Soto, five mares.

Don Gerardo Bojorges, one mare under three years old.

Don Natan N., thirty-two pesos which Senor Yncle took in beans with fifty calabazas llevadas por Jeremias [pumpkins carried by Jeremias].

Don Dolores Mesa, four fanegas [A Spanish measure of grain equal to 1.58

bushels] of wheat which I paid for him to Dona Concepcion Romero, now dead.

Don Mariano Martinez, five pesos, four given to him by my comrade Carmen; and one that I gave him.

Don Teodoro Flores, two fanegas of wheat

Item: I declare the following to be my property:
  Fifty head of cattle.
  Two yokes of oxen.
  One mule.
  Eight broken horses and a mare.
  A herd of six mares.
  Four axes, two with long handles, and two hatchets.
  One adze with a long handle, and one short one.
  A few carpenter tools.
  180 fanegas of wheat.
  Eight cart loads of corn in the ear.
  Eleven fanegas of beans.
  Two shotguns.
  Three plows fully equipped.

One piece of property which I have in the form of a loan, for which I have petitioned the Superior Departmental Government. I leave Don Antonio Buelna as my trustee in charge of this property.

Item: I declare that I owe the following:

To Rev. padre Fray Rafael Moreno for tithes of this year, twenty fanegas of wheat, eight of corn, ten arrobas [a bulk measurement equal to 25.36 pounds] of flour, and three fanegas of beans.

  One mass to Holy Mary and one to Saint Joseph.
  To Don Salvador Garcia, ten pesos.
  To Dona Concepcíon Romero, now dead, four fanegas of wheat and two steers.
  To Don Jose Maria Alviso, son-in-law of corporal Crisotomo, ten pesos.
  To Don Pedro Chavoya, two steers.
  To Don Antonio Chavoya, seven pesos.
  To Don Antonio Sunol, fourteen pesos.
  To Dona Dolores Vasquez, ten reales [a monetary unit; eight reales equaled one peso].
  To Dona Maria Archuleta, two pesos.

Item: I declare that I bought of William Richardson a piece of cloth, and paid for it three and half tercios [half a load] of flour, for which he has not yet rendered account.

Item: I leave as my legitimate heirs my wife, Dona Maria Antonia Mesa, and my children, Maria Luisa, Juan Capistrano, Maria de Jesus, Maria Francisca Cecilia, Maria Dolores, Juan Crisostomo, Francisco de las Llagas, Jose Guadalupe, Estevan, and one yet unborn.

Item: I name my wife Dona Maria Antonia Mesa, sole administrator of my assets, both those that I possess and those to be received.

I hereby revoke, annul, and declare of no value or effect any and all other wills or codicils that I may heretofore have made, since it is my will that this alone be valid and have effect in law and equity, and to this end I pray the Senor Alcalde of this jurisdiction to give this instrument the authorization necessary to make it legally valid.

And I, the constitutional Alcalde of the Pueblo of San Jose de Guadalupe, acting as receiver with two assisting witnesses in the absence of a notary public, do certify and declare that this will was executed as written, the testator being in his right mind and dictating its terms; and it shall be considered a public instrument with full force and value according to the will of the testator, notwithstanding the lack of certain legal requirements. It shall be filed in the archive of this tribunal, noting that for want of the properly stamped paper it is written on three sheets of common paper. Twentieth of February, Eighteen Hundred and Thirty Nine. Citizen Prado Mesa was a witness.

    Signed: *Jose Noriega* (rubric)
    Signed: *Jose Z Fernandez* (rubric) Assisting Witness
    Signed: *Salvio Pacheco* (rubric) Assisting Witness

APPENDIX VI

The Last Will and Testament of Joaquin Soto, 1852

On March 23, 1943, the *Monterey Peninsula Herald*, in an article by Beth Ingles, published the original handwritten will of Joaquin Soto. Listed as property in Joaquin's will are Rancho Del Piojo and the Monterey adobe home on Carmelo Street. The translation of this will, written in the colorful and dramatic style of the times, follows:

> In the name of Almighty God amen: I, Joaquin Soto, a native and citizen of the City of Monterey, legitimate son of the matrimony of Ysidoro [Isidoro] Soto and Marcela Linares, deceased, natives and citizens of the same place, by the divine mercy finding myself sick but being of sound mind, believing and confessing with firmament, I believe and confess in the mysteries of the Trinity, Father, Son and Holy Ghost, three distinct persons and only one true God, I believe in Holy Mary and our Lord Jesus Christ, that by the infinite merits of his precious life, passion, and death, will pardon all my faults and take me to enjoyment in his presence.
>
> Fearing the certainty of death which is natural to all human beings, I grant, order and make my testament in the following form. I commission my soul to God our Lord that from nothing he created and I order my corpse consigned to the earth from which it was formed and made me a cadaver. I want it enshrouded in the habit of Santo Domingo. It is my order that on the day of my funeral there shall be a High Mass Celebrated Cantado (sung) for the repose of my soul and with corpse present.
>
> I declare and recognize of my goods both real and personal property one home in Monterey situated between the Carmelo Road and the Sanjon (Gulch) of adobe with a tile roof and a lot of appertaining thereto with one hundred varas in every direction. I also declare that el Rancho Del Piojo, adjoining the ex-mission of San Antonio [near Jolon], consisting of Three Sitios de Granado Major (three square leagues of land for grown cattle) to be my property with a home on same of adobe with a tile roof, two corrals and one hundred head of tame cattle and five horses. I also declare to have in my possession, that is to say pledged (or mortgaged) seventy sheep (ewes) to Mr. Roach, sheriff, in the sum of two-hundred dollars on one and one-half months from the eleventh day of this month of September.

And also declare that Jose M. Villa owes me fifty dollars and two reses gordas (fat cattle or beef) as per a document I have in my possession, el Chino Rios, twenty dollars and Bonifacio Olivares, one tame cow; and also declare to be my debtor to Don Luis Lesse, ten dollars; to Don Maximo Taboas, thirteen and to Mr. Roach on account of the sheep (ewes) aforesaid two hundred dollars and also declare, coming to my memory, I have on the rancho Del Piojo, five yokes of oxen and three Spanish carts.

I declare that I am legitimately married with Dona Maria del Carmen Castro, legitimate daughter of Don Mariano Castro and Dona Josefa Romero. I declare to recognize our children of legitimate matrimony, Bernardino, Luisa, Barbara, Josefa, Lazaro, Jose Maria, Refugio, Augustine and Pedro. I declare for my only and universals heirs my said wife Dona Maria Carmel Castro and the nine children mentioned above and also declare this to be my last will that my wife goce y desfrute (enjoy and dispose) of one-third of my estate aforesaid and the other two-thirds part to be divided between nine said children share and share alike and without favor or betterment to any one over the others. And also declare and order that my said wife Dona Maria del Carmel Castro and my oldest son be executors and that my wife be tutor and guardian of the minors interin subsisto viuda (during her period of widowhood) but in case that contraiga nuevas mupsias (new marriage) then my second executor Bernardino shall take possession of that part of interest of the minors to be delivered when they are of competent age.

And lastly I order that at my death my executors can and should take possession of all my estate and property and to administer same without having to furnish any kind of bonds and I request of the Sir Judge, before whom these presents bring, approve and confirm these appointments and ratification of the aforesaid. And that it be with the benediction of God.

City of Monterey, of the State of California, the 13th day of September of the year one thousand eight hundred fifty two.
Joaquin Soto

Joaquin and Maria Del Carmen Soto had nine children who were necessary to operate their large land holdings. However, seven years after Joaquin's death, his wife was forced to sell Rancho El Piojo for payment of debts and to support her children. This would be the beginning of a series of unfortunate events that occurred to the Soto family and eventually to their grandson Count Soto.

GENERATION 4 (GENERAL)

Courtesy: Carol (Soto) Lowry

General Soto as a young man

General Herculeano Soto, son of Lazaro, was born on September 11, 1830, baptized at Mission San Juan Bautista, and was buried at the Cambria Catholic Cemetery in 1906.

An old story has been passed down through the generations regarding General Soto's boyhood. While fishing at age nine, he often walked without shoes until one day a fish bone pierced his foot. This hurt terribly, but not wanting to get into trouble because he was fishing instead of completing his chores, General never told his parents about the pain and injury to his foot. After several days of increasing swelling and severe pain, he was finally forced to tell his parents about his injured foot. His father, Lazaro, took him to a doctor, but by this time gangrene had set in. The doctor said there were no options but to amputate his foot and lower leg.

General was given whiskey (as a little boy, no less) to ease the pain and was told to chomp down on a piece of wood placed in his mouth, with the doctor wielding his knife and coarse handsaw to remove the foot and lower leg below the knee. General never let this slow him down. Physically, he was extremely strong. In fact, he's credited with building the road, using a team of horses, and putting up the adobe house on his 160-acre Adelaida homestead "Dry Bones." How difficult this must have been for a one-legged man! General used a hand-carved wooden peg on his amputated leg. Memories continue down through family members of General entertaining his grandchildren by playfully removing his peg leg and providing his constant tales of yesterday.

Early-day California was struggling politically with independence, causing great uncertainty among its people. The United States military forces were attempting to gain control of this potentially rich land. The United States flag was raised at the Custom House in Monterey on July 7, 1846, by Commodore John Drake Sloat. Although premature, a proclamation was issued which stated "Henceforth California will be a portion of the United States." Later in 1846, looking from the roof of the Presidio of Monterey, sixteen-year-old General witnessed United States military officer John Fremont carrying the United States flag through the streets of Monterey. This resulted in great apprehension for General. It proved to be a pivotal time in California's history since most Californios were not happy about statehood and remained loyal to Mexico. There was fear, which later proved to be accurate, that by joining the United States many personal possessions would be lost, including their beloved land.

Before 1860, General moved to the Green Valley area, south of Cambria, perhaps to be near relatives. General, age thirty, is listed in the San Luis Obispo County 1860 census as living in the same household with his thirty-year-old cousin Bernardino Soto. Jose Joaquin Bernardino Soto (1824-1900) was the oldest child of Maria del Carmen (Castro) Soto and Joaquin Soto. Bernardino was raised on the large 13,000-acre land grant of El Rancho El Piojo in Jolon, which was sold in 1859 to pay mounting family expenses.

Bernardino may have been the first Soto to move to the Cambria area. In 1855, Bernardino married Felicita (1837-c.1865), a local Indian woman in San Luis Obispo. It is unknown what happened to his wife, but she's listed as a mulatto housekeeper in the 1860 county census. This same 1860 census shows the Soto listing next to that of the Green family, a fact that implies they were neighbors in 1860.

Rufus Burnett Olmsted is credited in Annie Morrison and John Haydon's *History of San Luis Obispo County and Environs* (1917) as being the first Anglo in Green Valley in 1860. Olmsted moved onto land of Julian Estrada's Rancho Santa Rosa. A government survey was completed and Olmsted took possession of land once owned by Estrada. However, according to the 1860 census, both the Bernardino Soto and Samuel Green families were also living in upper Green Valley at the same time as the Olmsteds.

An intriguing account was uncovered while reviewing historian Paul Squibb's notes regarding the Green family, for whom the picturesque valley was named. After 1862, Samuel and Maria (Littlejohn) Green homesteaded 160 acres at Green Valley's headwaters on today's Negranti Ranch. Improvements of $3,000 were completed on the property, which were required under the Homestead Act regulations. Mr. Green died, however, on October 31, 1869, leaving his wife and several children to manage the homestead.

As mentioned, Bernardino Soto was a neighbor of the Green family for nearly a decade. It appears that he was quite active in business, inasmuch as he was involved in several mines near the Cambria area. In 1864-66, Bernardino filed a mining claim identified as "The Florinda Mine" along with partners Domingo Pujol, Joaquin Arques, Joaquin Estrada, Juan Castro, Esteram Castro, Samuel Green, and Juan Ricardo. The claim was described as 2,000-feet wide by 2,000-feet long for mining and prospecting purposes.

Prospecting on this new land was an occupation many of the early settlers believed would bring them wealth. Bernardino was involved in another claim identified as "Star of the West". This claim was to be mined for gold, silver, and copper. The company consisted of Bernardino, Samuel Green, James Van Ness, and George Hearst. As written by Hazel Olmsted in *Chronicles of Cambria's Pioneers* (1946):

> So far as is known, none of the claims recorded fulfilled their owners' expectations, and by 1870 the inhabitants in general had reached the realization that the real wealth of the region lay, not in mineral ledges, but in the fertility and productiveness of its soil.

In April 1870, Bernardino Soto, cousin to General, married the widow Maria (Littlejohn) Green. This second marriage of Bernardino lasted until the death of Maria on May 13, 1875, leaving questionable ownership of the Green property. Who now owned this land, her newly widowed husband, Bernardino Soto, or the Green children?

On June 16, 1881, Bernardino sold the property for $4,500 to Mr. Miles C. Marks. However, the property was not his to sell and the case ended up in San Luis Obispo County Superior Court. It also appeared that Samuel Green had established rights to the property but never legally filed for them. Because of this dispute, Bernardino left the Green Valley area and moved into the rugged terrain of Adelaida. This remote area, due east of San Simeon on the far side of the Santa Lucia Range, appeared to provide refuge to the Soto family during unsettled times when they could not understand the new Anglo laws.

During this same time-frame, General Soto moved to the Jolon area in southern Monterey County and acquired land. According to notes taken by Paul Squibb from an interview with a son of General, Joaquin "Jack" Soto, General owned and then lost land in the Mission San Antonio-Jolon area to the Atherton family in a land-swindling scheme.

In 1860, Faxon Dean Atherton (1815-1877) began his land acquisitions with the purchase of 640 acres at $10.00 per acre on the San Francisco peninsula. Atherton was a businessman and land speculator who purchased property in Hayward, Watsonville, and many other places. In 1875, Atherton bought Rancho Milpitas ("Little Fields") in the Jolon area from Ygnacio Pastor.

Ygnacio Pastor, a neophyte of Mission San Antonio, originally received the Mexican grant of Rancho Milpitas from Governor Alvarado on May 5, 1838. William Randolph Hearst's Piedmont Land and Cattle

Company later acquired this same rancho in 1922. In 1940, parts of this property were sold to the U.S. government as a training area now known as Fort Hunter Liggett.

Atherton purchased Rancho Milpitas immediately after its title clearance by the U.S. Land Commission in 1875. During the conversion of land, records under the land commission were altered and Pastor's small ranch mysteriously grew from a few thousand acres to 42,000 acres. According to Augusta Fink's *Monterey County: The Dramatic Story of Its Past (1972):*

> Atherton had acquired the old Rancho Milpitas, which stretched for many vaguely defined miles along the San Antonio River, and he claimed that the rancho comprised thousands of acres more than those recorded in the careless Mexican records.

Owners of plots dating back to the Hispanic period (including Indians, Mexicans, and Spaniards) who lived on land not originally owned by Pastor became "squatters" overnight. Atherton then sent out notice to evict all squatters. Many were settlers on improved lands awaiting pre-emption, and everyone in the Jolon area lost their property. Efforts at an appeal were taken to Washington, D.C., but proved unsuccessful. This was now Anglo law, and the Californios were unable to prove their historic ownership.

In 1877, Atherton's son was sent with the sheriff to evict all occupants and repossess their homes. Some of the wealthier occupants re-purchased their own properties, but most simply left the area.

This maneuver by Atherton eliminated General Soto's claim to his property in the Jolon area, also forcing him to relocate. General, as a result of having his Jolon property "stolen," greatly mistrusted the Yankees and their laws. This distrust of Americans remained constant for the rest of his life. He then moved into the remote mountains of Adelaida, well south of Jolon, where his goats could roam on public lands, as long as public lands were available. It was during this period that General homesteaded the Dry Bones property in Adelaida, west of present-day Paso Robles.

Little information on General's first wife is available. General married in 1861, and his wife died in about 1866. This marriage produced one son, Joseph Soto (1866-1920), who married Eveline Osorio in 1887 and then Avelina "Lilly" Soria (1876-1962) in 1901. It's believed Joe Soto worked as a vaquero and warehouseman on the Hearst Ranch in San Simeon for twenty-five years. According to the 1910 San Luis Obispo County census, Joe and Lilly had five children.

Some family members believe that after the death of General's first wife, a girl was brought in to assist in raising young Joe Soto. This young woman was identified as "Lola G." in the 1870 San Antonio Township census of Monterey County. Could the letter "G" represent Grajalva? Since Lola is the common nickname for Dolores, it seems likely that this woman became General's second wife. Because Lola's occupation was listed as homemaker in the census, she may have been married to General at this time.

About 1869, General's second marriage was to Dolores Grajalva (1856-1923). The Grajalva family made their money from mining and later purchased ten acres of land adjacent to Mission Dolores in San Francisco. This second marriage of General to Dolores produced seven children.

The first child from this second marriage was Cipriano Soto. This same 1870 Monterey census shows young Cipriano as being nine months old, indicating that he was actually born in September of 1869, not 1870 as sometimes recorded. However, it may never be possible to answer all the questions concerning General and his early life before he homesteaded the Dry Bones Ranch in Adelaida.

Because General's father, Lazaro, was baptized in 1801 at nearby Mission San Antonio, General must have been familiar with the Central Coast area. General is credited with homesteading 160 acres in the Adelaida area that served as the basis for the Cambria branch of the Soto family. It's believed that the paperwork was not completed correctly when this parcel was first homesteaded, probably in the 1870s (remember they didn't speak English). Yet, as late as 1898, under President William McKinley, this land was formally filed for under the Homestead Act of 1862. It was Homestead Certificate No. 6405, application 10,818. This 160-acre parcel, known as Dry Bones passed down to family members for several generations until it became too cumbersome to retain. As previously mentioned, the name Dry Bones was given to this land in reference to the many dry, bleached bones of dead animals that littered the ground after the great drought of 1862-64. On October 25, 1971, the property was sold to the Natoma Council of Camp Fire Girls. The Central Coast Council of Camp Fire U.S.A. is now headquartered in Pismo Beach.

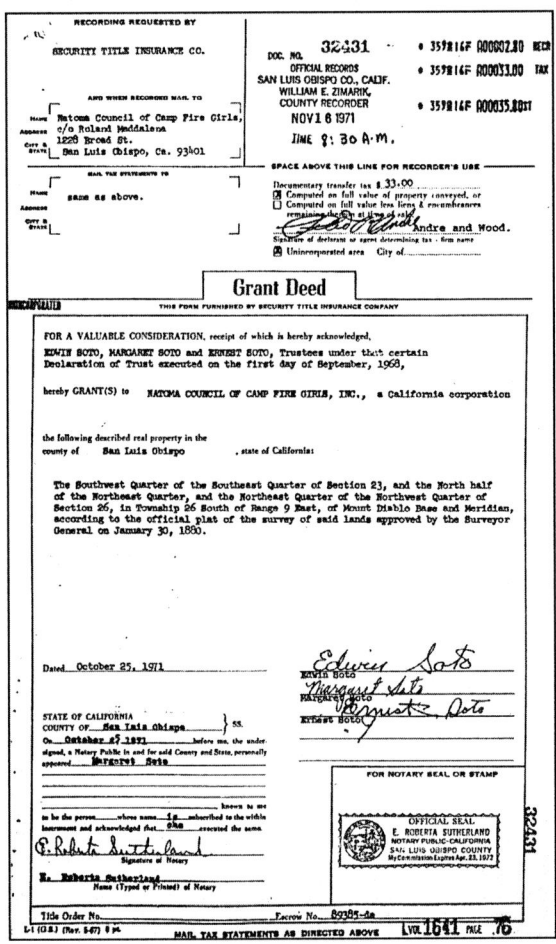

Courtesy: Robert Soto
Grant Deed to Natoma Campfire Girls

The difficult times during the great drought of the early 1860s are well documented. As Delmar Williams wrote in *Chronicles of Cambria's Pioneers* (1946):

> The vicissitudes suffered by the Olmsteds in their Green Valley log house would try the soul of the bravest pioneer. Soon after their arrival came the driest of all dry years in the State of California, the year of 1863 and '64. A little rain fell in November of 1863 but not another drop came down until Pluvius sent a shower in April of 1864. Thru-out San Luis Obispo County cattle and horses died of starvation by the thousands. In a last effort to save their cattle and horses, the Olmsted boys drove them into the mountains above San Carpojo [north of San Simeon]; however only sixteen survived.

On one occasion having no horse, Mr. Olmsted carried a fifty pound sack of flour on his back from San Simeon to his Green Valley ranch. Clams, which the boys toted over the hills from Morro Bay, furnished a large portion of the family diet.

Leonard Pitt's book *The Decline of the Californios* states:

A quarter of the state's wealth crumbled from 1862 to 1864, including as much as 40 per cent of its livestock, with the main devastation occurring in the south. Santa Barbara had 200,000 head of cattle in 1862, a mere 5,000 in 1865. Ranchers there auctioned 50,000 head of cattle in 1862 at 37½ cents a head in April, 1864, the lowest price ever; even in the Mexican days hide and carcass each had brought a dollar.

For many ranching families, 1864 meant the end of solvency; their names generally went on the delinquent tax list and stayed there until they had sold their property. Before the catastrophe, practically all land parcels worth more than $10,000 had still been in the hands of old families; by 1870, these families held barely one-quarter.

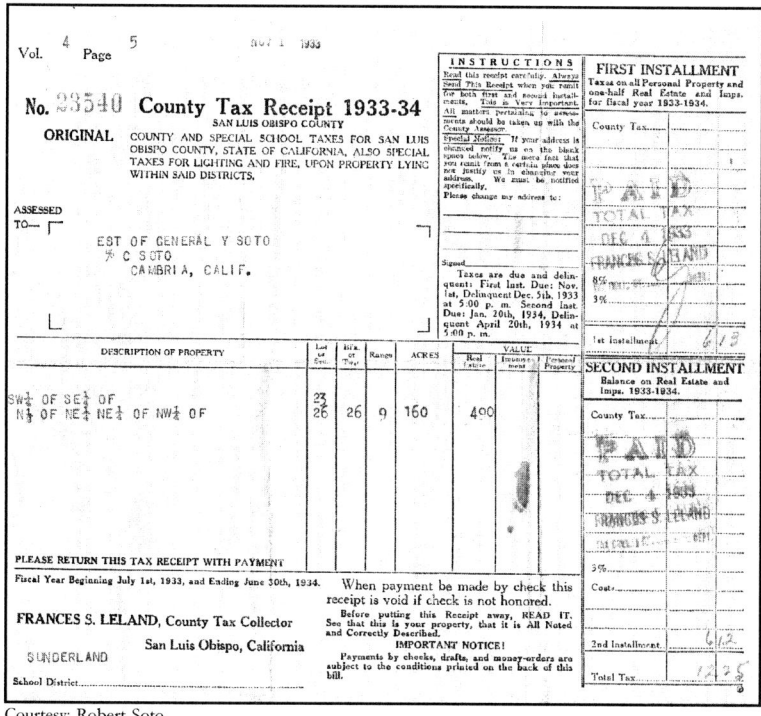

Courtesy: Robert Soto

1933-34 Property Tax Bill from Dry Bones

Courtesy: Steven Soto
Young Vernon Soto with Ernest (top photo) and Elsie (bottom photo) on porch of Dry Bones Adobe; 1936

On July 1 and July 4, 1957, Jack Soto's neighbor Paul Squibb interviewed him about his early memories and family stories:

Jack Soto says his father [General Soto] remembered the Americans landing at Monterey and the raising of Stars and Stripes. He never would learn English. Near Klau mine they were surrounded by English-speaking people, but there were plenty of Spanish and Indian people at Jolon. His father [b. 1832] used to talk about the 1864 drought. Jack thinks he carried only one horse through, with corn stalks off the roof. In 1898, they got pretty good feed in the mountains, but people from the drier country drove cattle to the mountains. They cut oak for leaves, moss and mistletoe for the cattle.

The elder daughter of General, Braulia Soto, also homesteaded a parcel in the Dry Bones-Adelaida area. Records indicate that on February 13, 1905, Braulia homesteaded land adjacent to General. Her parcel was Township 0260S, Range 0090E, and Section 035. In 1907, Braulia married Ed Spooner, whose parents were Alden Bradford Spooner and Roxana (Gilmore) Spooner. The Spooner family settled in the Montano de Oro area west of Los Osos on property now known as Spooner's Cove.

The Botts family, a neighboring family in the Adelaida area, recalled dining with the General Soto family. Joe Botts tells a story of his grandfather eating supper with the Soto family in Dry Bones. This evening meal made a lasting impression on the Botts family and has been handed down for three generations. When it was time to sit down at the dinner table, each person stood by their chair until all the food was placed on the table by Dolores, who was addressed as "La Senora" (the lady). When Dolores brought the last serving plate, she was seated first, and then everyone else took a seat. This tradition was one of respect for "the lady" who cooked the meals and took care of the family.

Francis Rademacker, a close friend of the Soto family, made an early 1950s tape-recording of family stories, an account that's greatly treasured. These tapes recorded the voices of Cipriano, Ernest, Andrew, and Edwin Soto. Edward Frank "Ponch" Asabez, son of Edward Asabez (1911-1954), was also interviewed and told fascinating family stories about General and Dolores Soto, who were his grandparents.

Ponch Asabez tells of the old Soto adobe home at Dry Bones. Dolores was considered one of the best cooks around the area. She had the knack for making a big tasty meal when there was little food available. If a shotgun shell was found on the kitchen shelf, she would send out one of her boys to shoot quail for dinner. If they were able to kill only one or two birds, she would make a hearty quail soup. Rice, potatoes, onions, quail, and whatever else was available were thrown into the pot. After adding the seasoning from the large wooden spice containers stored in the kitchen, the boiling hot soup was ready. Nearly all meals were served with homemade tortillas, which helped fill an empty stomach. It never mattered if five or fifteen people were present for dinner; there was always enough food, even in those difficult times. Today, my cousin John Lowry has the original cast iron cooking pot that came from the Soto adobe. This unique pot had a large handle so it could be hung from a steel rod in the open fireplace.

There was also an open ring on the side of the pot to swing it over and out of the fire for stirring or serving.

The gregarious Ponch Asabez described the Christmas holiday season at the Soto home in Dry Bones. In preparation for this event, Dolores would cook for several days. Typical food would be turkey, chicken, enchiladas, tamales, tortillas, and even a small stuffed pig. The party lasted for seven days, from Christmas through New Year's Day. Enough food was prepared to last the entire week. The table was always set with silverware and plates so anyone could come in and eat at any time. In fact, if neighbors stopped by and no one was home, they were expected to sit down and eat. Perhaps a note would be left thanking Dolores for the meal, but if not a note, they could just thank her the next time they saw her.

During the late 1800s there were no locks on any door—in fact, no locks at all. Honesty and respect were commonplace in the country. Neighbors, friends, and, of course, family were always welcome at the Soto adobe. The special Christmas holiday always meant food, music, and dancing. Music was a very important form of entertainment since many family members played instruments.

Another interesting account told by Ponch Asabez was one regarding General Soto. It seems he had three or four milk cows at the homestead. One day he decided to sell cream to the townsfolk so he could make a little extra money. General milked his cows and separated the cream off the top. He then carefully poured this cream into containers, which were tied by leather straps onto his saddle horn. General rode off to deliver this precious cream to the Klau Mine, where the stagecoach stopped every day. The stage driver would pick up the cream and take it to Paso Robles, where it was sold. After about two weeks, the stage returned to the Klau Mine with General's eight dollars for the cream. This was a fortune for General. What easy money! After receiving more cream money, General went to Paso Robles and bought a second-hand cream separator to increase the amount of cream production and provide extra money for his large family.

In an interview by Paul Squibb recalling General Soto's early life, his son Jack Soto spoke of playing music in a special band:

> Jack Soto says there was a Spanish-speaking orchestra in Jolon that used to play at Cambria, San Simeon, and other places when he was a boy and young man, one of them was his uncle. 2 violins, a flute and a guitar, and a cornet, though he does not remember the latter (cornet) coming to Cambria.

They would ride over on horseback and the hotel would put them up free. They would get 5 or 6 dollars apiece. Jack played with them sometimes. The dances were held in Rigdon Hall, [the two-story Rigdon Hall building was next to Soto's Market] which is now the movie [theater], was then the loft of a blacksmith shop. Dances would begin early and last till daylight—sometimes. They never used written music.

Courtesy: Karen (Soto) Snow
San Antonio Band members with Louisa and Barney Soto in back row, standing in front of Cambria's Ridgon Hall; circa 1906

Jack's story was collaborated in Geneva Hamilton's *Where the Highway Ends* (1974); the band was known as the San Antonio Band:

It [the San Antonio Band] was considered the last word in musical excellence. It was first introduced to the Cambria area by his father [General], who rode over with them from time to time. His father was a great joker. Once he hid all the musician's instruments in the various bars of the town. They were compelled to perform in each bar in order to redeem the instruments. At another time, because he disapproved of the dirty clothes the musicians were wearing, he caused their clothes to be badly burned as they dried on a log near a camp fire while they slept. Awaking in the morning they had only burned rags for clothes. On arrival in Cambria

Yrculano [General] told the sad tale of burned clothes to the local merchants with such pathos they were induced to supply the nearly naked men with new blue jeans.

Regular members of the band were Manuel Rosas, flute; Pedro Moreno, second violin; Celestino Garcia, guitar; and Jose Maria Caravajales, first violin. Occasionally they also had a cornetist. The men were always lodged free of charge at the local hotels. Jack always played guitar with the group whenever they came to the area. In later years he played with local musicians, the Van Gorden boys, Frank Mayfield, George Allen and Francisco "Poncho" Estrada, continuing to do so for over 30 years.

Jim Soto, a great-grandson of General, has one of the original Colt .36 caliber pistols once owned by General. In later years, the Dry Bones adobe home was broken into and vandalized. Since General was poor and did not have many possessions, there was not much to steal. However, General did have a matching set of right- and left-handed Colt pistols dated 1850 and two long guns, which were kept in the adobe. The thieves stole the rifles and the right-handed pistol. Fortunately, at the time of this robbery, General had the left-handed pistol in his possession. This Colt is

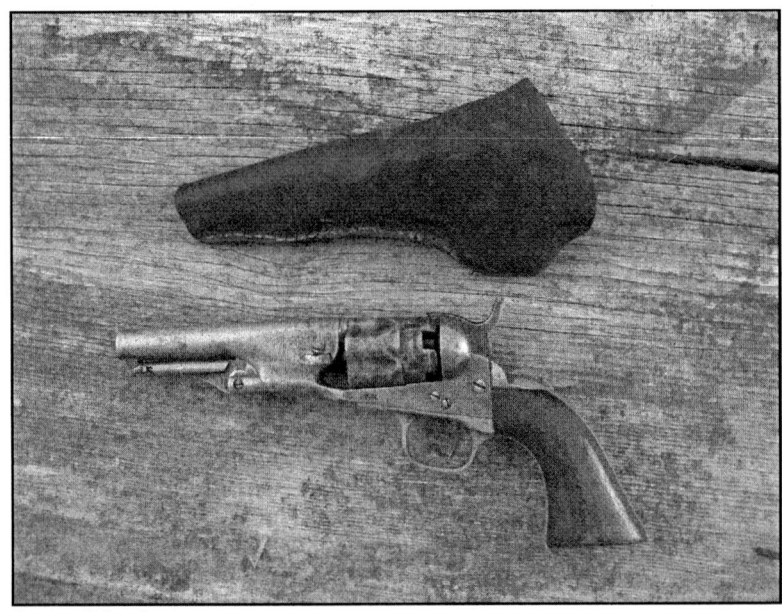

Courtesy: Robert Soto

**General's 1850 Colt .36 caliber
5-shot Revolver Pistol**

a five-shot revolver, cap-and-ball pistol. The rear sight is a groove cut into the hammer, which lines up with a small ball on the end of the short barrel. It's believed that this was the left-handed pistol because of its leather holster that allowed it to be carried on the left hip. It has been said that General always carried this pistol with him. The pistol is identified as the "Sheriff" model by Colt. Cipriano saved the left-handed Colt and gave it to Jim Soto, who treasures it today. This is one of the few items remaining (except photos) from General's time at Dry Bones.

In 1906, when General was elderly and became sick, his family brought him through the hills from Adelaida into Cambria to see the doctor. A horse was used with a makeshift Indian-type carrying device, known as a travois, to transport General, who was unable to walk. What a trip that must have been through the rough mountainous terrain and across the many streams! General never returned home, and he died in Cambria at the age of seventy-four. Today, General rests in the old Catholic cemetery on the hill overlooking Cambria, as the eldest patriarch of the Cambria branch of the Soto family.

General Herculeano Soto had seven children with Maria Dolores (Grajalva) Soto. The children were:

1. **Cipriano Soto** b. 1869/70 d. 1956
   m. 1895 Carmel Asebez b. 1879 d. 1964
2. Braulia Soto b. 1872 d. 1934
   m. 1907 Edmund L. Spooner b. 1869 d. 1908
3. Augustine "Gus" Soto b. 1875 d. 1947
   m. 1898 Mary Warren b. 1877 d. 1956
   m. 1923 Lilly Messic b. 1893 d. 1947
4. Bernardino "Barney" Soto b. 1879 d. 1950
   m. 1902 Margaret Ingles b. 1878 d. 1958
5. Mary Francisca Soto b. 1879 d. 1894
6. Joaquin "Jack" Modesto Soto b. 1886 d. 1981
   m. 1910 Agnes Maggetti b. 1888 d. 1976
   (Jack – began Soto's Market in Cambria)
7. Louisa "Beva" Soto b. 1890 d. 1969
   m. 1910 Edward Asebez b. 1872 d. 1932
   m. 1944 Morie Barba b. 1886 d. 1960

APPENDIX VII

Dry Bones

Much information is available on life at Dry Bones thanks to the Cambria Historical Society. Paul Squibb's notes on General's youngest son, Jack Soto, and their excursion into Dry Bones in 1961, reveal insights into the hardships of life for General's family. Because this information is handwritten and often difficult to read, several areas have been noted with question marks (?) where it was impossible to decipher Paul Squibb's handwritten notes.

Soto Ranch - Dry Bones Trip
July 8, 1961
by
Paul Squibb
(Interview of Joaquin "Jack" Soto)

After many attempts a trip to Drybones Country with L.G.S. [Louise Squibb], P.S. [Paul Squibb], Joaquin Modesto Soto, and Agnes Maggetti Soto finally got underway, 8:15 a.m., via Santa Rosa Creek, which was beautiful for early mists (7:15 standard time) with covey after covey of quail.

Jack (aged 76!) was especially full of remembrance, Aggie somewhat. It is hard to remember such a flood of incidents, mostly personal and trivial.

Aggie said her parents (?) lived in a house on the north side of creek, above the Highway 1 bridge (now Main Street). She repeated Mabel Brights' assertion that there was a house [the house was below Scott Rock, across from the football stadium] in the little cove of Eucalyptus trees, on north side of road, as it starts towards [Coast Union] High School. Then, of course, she mentioned the Scott house, whose cellar-hole can still be seen below Scott Rock, in grove of Eucalyptus, on knoll, barn now vanishing from sight.

From that house by creek Aggie rode a bicycle once a week to Gamboni's Ranch to do the washing.

Jack said Rafael Mora was Spanish-speaking like us and we always took his word for the value of cattle. He made money buying cattle. The boys have borrowed money on the land R. (Rafael) owned clear. Christine Jack is known by Jack and Aggie as Mrs. Jack, because she had a son. Vernon

Soto and [Bob] Lowry lease a pasture [7X Ranch] between 7X Dee Fitzhugh and Nick Marquart place. The stream always had great trout. It would seem to flow from Fitzhugh corral on top of ridge southeastward.

Starting down toward Las Tablas Creek, we found the road all chewed up and dusty from work at about the old mining project near summit. Jack said Ed Biaggini Jr. is doing it and that he also is doing the work at Klau Mine (or whatever is the proper name for the mine and still nearest Sunderland School).

Jack returned to that region after he was married, 1909, '10, and '11 (somewhat hazy) and lived at his father's place (died 1906). He worked at Klau Mine for a while and was fired, he thinks, because he stammered in talking with manager, who stammered. The latter apparently thought he was being mocked. We stopped briefly at 7X headquarters. And saw Mrs. Dee [Minabelle] Fitzhugh, who was just going out. She was a Phillips from the west side of the mtns [mountains], daughter of the women L. [Louise] has met with Brights in Cayucos.

There was a Carmen family, who lived in Carmen Creek, just below 7X. They used to hold barbecues and the Soto's used to ride over.

Jack and other children appear to have attended school (Oak Flat?) no longer in existence. There was a tannery briefly not far south of Marion Davis' Ranch and entry to Camp Natoma. The man sold stock to a number of local people, built some stone vats, made a little ? leather, and then gave up. (There is considerable tan-oak on the east slope, beside black, white, blue, canyon and coast live oaks.) The location Jack pointed out showed no sign of stone structures.

A Marion Davis child assured us the gates were open. We found Davis at the attractive but vacant house about half-way to Camp Natoma. He was feeding a large bunch of recently weaned calves. He seems like a hard worker and is apparently doing well.

The road makes bad going for our new Chevrolet Corvair, with engine in rear and uniformly low clearance, also a valve not working and consequent loss of power. Louise managed to get us all the way in without hitting bottom.

A group of campfire girls were at Camp Natoma. One of the women in charge was Mrs. Went ? [Wentz] one of the Gregg girls from Stepladder Ranch, in San Simeon Creek. (Others were Mrs. Goodall of Cambria, Mrs. Evans of Morro-Atascadero Rd., Mrs. Wentz of Stepladder Ranch.)

We left the car and Aggie at the camp, and Jack, Louise, and I walked slowly up the washed-out road to the Soto homestead, perhaps two miles, with typical hot sun and dry air. There were occasional pools of water in the creek, and considerable bird-life and a few interesting bushes; but the main thing to think about was "Dry Bones" Ranch.

Jack showed us where the team ran away on the awful day when as a boy he gambled away in Paso Robles the family's cash for perhaps a month's provisions. The wagon stayed right side up until the team reached a little flat they call the big depot, and there they dumped the provisions Jack had got on tick [credit] and smashed the wagon. His father wanted to take an axe to what was left of the wagon, but apparently did not do so. Jack's mother had a little stashed away, here and there, and appears to have smoothed matters over for Jack. She was something of a midwife and earned some money. Something like once a month, somebody had to drive, all day, to Paso Robles, spend the night, and drive back all the next day. But when the creek was up, as much of the rainy season, they just forgot about getting out at all.

Jack's father, known as General Yrculano [Herculeano] Soto was squeezed out of his land holdings near Jolon (probably by the Atherton Crowding (?) based on an original swindle in the form of raising a grant from 4,000 acres to 40,000).

Jack told me for the first time today that his father also tried to take up land in Green Valley after leaving Jolon. (He probably settled on Estrada land and was pushed out by George Hearst 1866-69. *The Pioneer* of 1869 mentions Hearst as having launched a lot of litigation harmful to the country in the past 3 years.)

It would seem that General Y. Soto, with one leg and such smoldering resentment toward Yankees that he would never speak English, took up 160 acres of government land at "Drybones" during the seventies [1870s]. His brother, Bernardino, [actually cousin] also homesteaded adjacent [to General]. Jack and his sister, later Mrs. Acebes [Asabez], for a while owned present Camp Natoma. But I am not clear whether Augustine, Barney and Cipriano ever did so. Jack was born at Drybones 1886. The older sister, who later married Spooner, seems to have filed in a quarter section.

I believe Jack and one sister were born at Drybones and the others elsewhere and previous to 1880. One girl died at about age 15 and was buried in Adelaida cemetery.

The "General" was born 1832, as best they could tell. Jack's mother was his second wife and much younger.

As the place appears now, it is steep and spectacularly rocky, and still difficult of access, through by air-line it is absurdly near Lime Mountain [northwest of Dry Bones] and other points that are reached by road. The hayfields, which they mowed with scythes, are pathetically small and are reduced by recent gullying and creek erosion. The site of the adobe house was cramped and steep, though disguised recently by Ernest Soto, who bulldozed the adobe away and prepared a relatively large building-site. A half-dozen pear trees remain and a small barn of pole and shake construction. Many smaller structures – chicken house, goat corral, etc. have entirely disappeared. But there are many vestiges of a fence of oak staves, split at enormous effort and fastened to a strand of heavy smooth wire to form an enclosure for the buildings and orchard. El General, probably with good help from the older boys, labored prodigiously to form the adobe bricks, roof the house mainly with poles and shakes, build the other buildings and fences, box in the excellent spring with redwood planks, provide a small pond and side-hill ditches to water some fruit trees and a small garden. There was also a pond for the ducks, filled from a smaller spring.

And the place was alive with ducks, geese, turkeys, and chickens, in Jack's boyhood memory. They always had plenty to eat, with the birds laying eggs in the barn and sheds and little haystacks and raising broods hap-hazard. The poultry roosted in the chicken house and thus seems to have escaped the bobcats, coyotes, skunks, coons, owls and perhaps other predators. There were usually 3 dogs to help. Jack "used to" go after bobcats with the dogs, and when they treed, the boys "used to" knock them out of the tree with stones.

Everyone helped milk the dozen or so of cows, which provided milk, butter and cheese of some sort for the family and all the animals. They usually did not sell either butter or cheese. Friends would move in to visit them at times and would camp beside the creek, a stone's throw from the house. No doubt the friends got all the dairy products they could use, and meat, too, when an animal was killed.

They usually milked some goats too, though I judge the 200 or so goats were mostly loose in the craggy hills. The goats seem to have been the main cash crop, for they sold goats to the Klau mine for $1.50 apiece, never more nor less. The Sotos enjoyed goat meat too and could slaughter such small animals without much waste in hot weather. Jack used to be sent out on a horse to bring the goats in, sometime from as far as Lime Mountain and other rough spots. When he started the flock toward home they kept going very well. The females were easy to get in to give birth to their kids. Predators in the hills must have been a problem. Once a lion got into the corral and killed 7. El General poisoned one of the carcasses and apparently killed the lion, for they followed the tracks and saw where spasms (strychnine?) had caused it to thrash the brush.

The cows were mixed dairy types, but not black-and-white. They kept a red bull, probably Durham. They did not slaughter calves. Grown steers were killed at any time of year. They ate tongue, heart, and liver, and they corned some in brine or saltpeter; but most of the meat they dried as jerky. They seem not to have cooperated with neighbors in slaughtering – as would have made for more fresh meat, especially in hot weather.

There was always a few horses, of course, for riding and driving the long way to Adelaida store and post office, where they went perhaps every two weeks and for the much longer two-day trips to El Paso de los Robles. They kept bells on a few of the animals. Considering the cramped little fields, the best of which was fenced with oak pickets, to include the house, and another later with barbed wire to protect perhaps two acres of hay, the six horses, twelve cows, a number of calves, steers, the bull, and as many as 200 goats, not to mention the poultry and a few hogs (which were perhaps penned up and fed skimmed milk) must have made short work of the feed within sight of the house. The animals must have strayed to every corner and crag within a mile. In the worst seasons, the Sotos would cut tree limbs to carry the animals through on leaves and Spanish moss. It could have been no bed of roses, even in a good season.

This day was piping hot. Louise drove us, with some difficulty in Chevrolet Covair, 1 valve not working, over Black Mt. and down Las Tablas. At Camp Natoma, Aggie stayed with car and Jack (aged 76) and Louise and I staggered 2 fairly rough miles, uphill to Drybones, where Jack showed us everything near house-site and we sat and drank water at spring. By the end of 3 hours we were back at car at Natoma and enjoyed Soto's fried chicken and watermelon and food and drink of ours. When we started out for home I drove slowly, with valve tapping badly. It was all caution but not enough judgment, I banged the front end on a rock and broke the gas line. Long before we reached the top of the first long hill, the gas was gone. We sat by the road in the heat and dust and wondered what to do.

I walked back a mile or more to the camp. Young Deugata (sp?) and a boy from SLO (Fitzhugh?) who were helping at camp cheerfully got out [of] the truck [with] and rope and water and drove me back up the dusty hill.

But at the car we found the young Louis and a friend, Mr. Alf Starkie, with some kids in a station wagon. Mr. Starkie was already under our car taping our broken tube together.

The boys took some gas from the camp's truck. To my surprise the tubing held fairly well and we were able to drive on up the hill, followed by the boys in the truck. We made it to the old Smiths (sp?) house and had a pleasant call on the Gillaways (sp?), formerly of Los Olivos, who provided further gas, which got us home.

I gave the boys $5, partly for the good of the camp and partly for value received. But Mr. Starkie provided the talent that actually got us out of a bad situation. I thanked him profusely by letter.

On way between Marion Davis Ranch and Camp Natoma we stopped and talked with Mr. Bill (?) Clausen and a boy and a Mexican who spoke no English.

Jack and Aggie exchanged civilities with the latter especially. He appears an educated Mexican, working for an uncle who has a tamale factory in Los Angeles.

These 3 were on horseback with sacks of #1080 squirrel poison – frightful stuff that the agricultural commissioner has allowed only in hands of very reliable men. This appears the beginning of a poison program that may have dire results for the county.

Paul Squibb
Cambria

GENERATION 5 (CIPRIANO)

Courtesy: Robert Soto

Cipriano Soto mounted on his horse

Cipriano Soto was born at Jolon on September 16, 1870. He died in 1956 while living in Harmony, south of Cambria. Cipriano was the eldest son of General Herculeano Soto and his second wife, Maria Dolores Grahalva. At age twenty-four, Cipriano married Carmel Irene Asabez; the date was May 11, 1895. Carmel was only fifteen years old at the time of her wedding, and she was required to obtain parental permission for the marriage. Cipriano and Carmel had three children, all born on the Hearst Ranch in San Simeon.

The eldest child was Andrew Asebez Soto; born in 1896, he died in 1973 and was married twice. His first wife was Violet Ingles (1903-1938). His second wife, Lucylle Wagner (1913-2000), worked at the San Simeon

Courtesy: Robert Soto

Asebez Family; 1884

Post Office for many years with Postmaster Pete Sebastian. Ernest Cipriano Soto, the second born (1899-1979), married Elsie Letticia Barlogio (1905-1989), who is buried in the Cambria Catholic Cemetery next to Ernest. Evelyn Soto was the last child (1900-1995). She was never married and was taken care of by her mother, Carmel.

Courtesy: Karen (Soto) Snow
Family Cowboys at Dry Bones Homestead: Augustine Soto, Joaquin Soto, Ed Asebez, Cipriano Soto and Bernardino Soto

Cipriano was raised in the hills of Adelaida with his family. Being the oldest brother, there were always many chores for him. At seventeen years of age he began working for the Hearst Ranch in San Simeon. While working for the Hearsts, Cipriano earned $25.00 per month and was able to save a little money. The ties to San Simeon and the Hearsts would remain throughout Cipriano's entire life since he did not venture far from this coastal area.

In the late 1880s, many years before the construction began at Hearst Castle, Cipriano was the coachman for Phoebe Apperson Hearst. Cipriano was responsible for transporting Mrs. Hearst around the county in a coach with a team of four horses. Mrs. Hearst was always very respectful and kind to Cipriano, no doubt thankful for his care and skill with the horses. Often Cipriano would take Mrs. Hearst and her guests to the train station, church, or other places in San Luis Obispo. All the trips tended to be a full day's journey, occasionally requiring a lunch stop near the "willows" around Morro Bay (near the present-day high school and Cloisters development).

An oral history interview of Cipriano's son Ernest Soto, conducted by granddaughter Shirlene Soto on January 29, 1978, reveals:

> Mrs. Hearst was very good to him [Cipriano] and his family; in fact she would give him a dollar tip many times, sometimes even $5 when he had to go to San Luis Obispo to meet the train.

On these trips Mrs. Hearst always asked Cipriano if he wished to share in her specially packed lunch. Cipriano would typically decline the offer since his duty was to take care of the four-horse team.

Grandson Jim Soto recalls the story of Cipriano attending first grade in Green Valley's Olmstead School. (This information and timing is confirmed in Paul Squibb's notes on "Dry Bones" when Jack Soto mentioned that his father, General, moved to Green Valley before homesteading in Adelaida.) Cipriano and his family spoke Spanish only, not English. On Cipriano's first day of school at Olmstead, the other children made fun of him because they couldn't understand his language. Cipriano was so embarrassed that he refused to return to school until he learned English. This was his first day of formal schooling, but it was also his last. He never returned to school again. He learned to read and write from a neighbor who spoke English. As with many people of this generation, Cipriano learned beautiful penmanship. He took pride in the artistic signing of his name and can be remembered practicing his "loops" before placing the pen to paper.

Cipriano's and Carmel's Signatures

On September 11, 1949, Cipriano wisely hand wrote a document identifying where he and Carmel had lived beginning with San Simeon. In 1895, Phoebe Apperson Hearst had a special home constructed for newlyweds Cipriano and Carmel, which was located near the large barn across the driveway from the old George Hearst "Senator's house." It's believed that Phoebe wanted to show her gratitude and respect to Cipriano by building this home. This small ranch house was where Cipriano's three children were born.

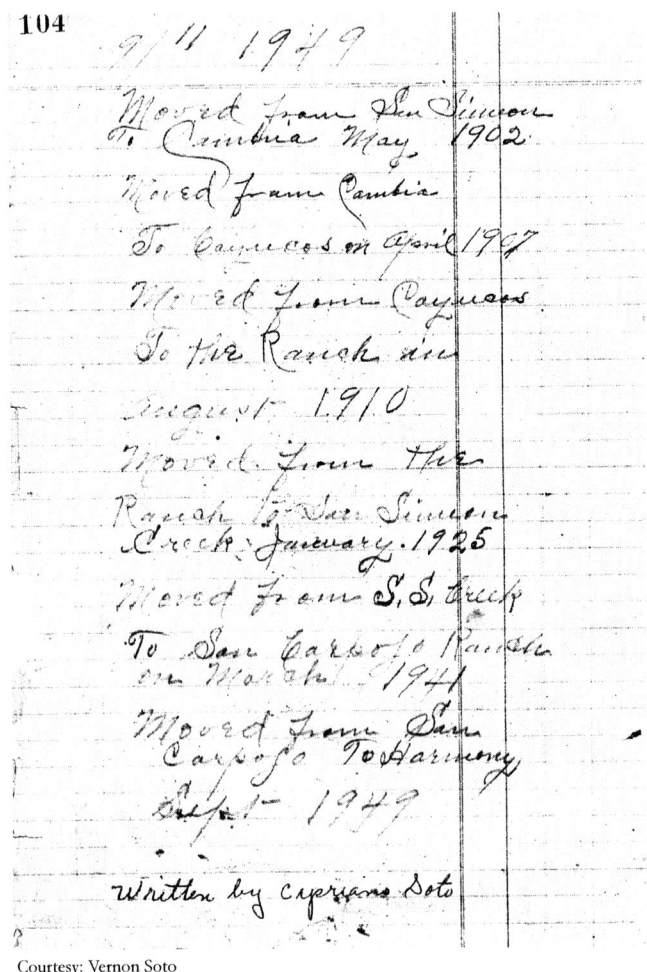

Courtesy: Vernon Soto
Cipriano's Handwritten Notes of Places Lived

San Simeon was a growing community thanks to George Hearst. Anastacio Asebez, father of Carmel, operated a butcher shop in early San Simeon. He taught the family the trade of slaughtering and butchering animals. A San Luis Obispo *Tribune* article dated October, 26, 1883 mentions San Simeon and the meat market located at the south end of town, near the small creek:

> We have here an excellent hotel and two stores filled with general merchandise, containing everything needful from a pocket knife to a silk dress. And our beef, we think it better, year in and year out than in any other place in the State. Mr. Asebez furnishes us with porterhouse, sirloin and all parts of beef at ten cents per pound and purchasers come here from Cambria, ten miles away, and from an equal distance in other directions, except off on the ocean.

In May 1902 the Soto family moved to Cambria. While living there for five years, Cipriano worked for his relatives as a butcher. The business was owned by Mora, Hitchcock, Asebez, and Ford. Edward Asebez was Carmel's elder brother. Cipriano's younger sister Louisa Mayo "Beva" Soto married Edward Asebez on September 14, 1910. Brother and sister, Cipriano and Beva Soto, married sister and brother, Carmel and Ed Asebez. The Cambria butcher shop was on the corner of Bridge Street and Proctor Lane, where Pacific Bell is now situated (across the street from the U.S. Post Office). From Cambria, they relocated to Cayucos in April 1907. After living in Cayucos, where Cipriano operated a meat market for the same owners as in Cambria, they moved to the newly purchased home ranch (the Ivans place) on upper Santa Rosa Creek in August 1910.

In January 1925, when Cipriano's boys, Andrew and Ernest, were old enough to operate the ranch, Cipriano went back to work at the Hearst Ranch, moving to San Simeon Creek (the present-day Pedotti Ranch). Leaving the Hearst house on San Simeon Creek in March 1941, the family again moved to another Hearst property, this time at San Carpojo Creek. Cipriano and Carmel's last move was from San Carpojo to Harmony on the Filos and Walter Ranch in September 1949.

As documented in Morrison and Haydon's *San Luis Obispo County and Environs*:

> Edward Asebez was married to Miss Louisa Soto, a native of this county, who was born at Adelaida, the daughter of General Soto, born in Monterey, who was a farmer and stockman, and settled in Adelaida, but returned to Cambria, where he died. Her mother had been Dolores Grahalva, a native of San Francisco, and the daughter of John Grahalva, who came from Mexico

as a gold seeker, and who, finding what he sought, bought ten acres of land near the Dolores Mission, where he engaged in business. He later moved to Jolon, Monterey County, where he died, and where Dolores was married. His wife was Theresa Morano, a native of Mexico, who died in Belmont. General Soto died in Cambria in 1906. His widow still owns the farm at Adelaida, but makes her home in Paso Robles with her daughter, Mrs. Asebez.

After his marriage, Mr. Asebez bought, with his brother-in-law, Cipriano Soto, the ranch on Santa Rosa creek, which they still own and conduct under the personal charge of Mr. Soto.

Chas. H. Ivins et ux : THIS INDENTURE, Made this eighth day of August in the year of
TO : our Lord nineteen hundred and ten BETWEEN H. H. Carpenter and
Ed. Asebez et al : Irene J. Carpenter, his wife, and Charles H. Ivins and Maude A.
: Ivins, his wife, of the County of San Luis Obispo, California,
the part- of the first part, and Ed. Asebez and Cipriano Soto of the same County and
State the parties of the second part, WITNESSETH: That the said parties of the first
part, for and in consideration of the sum of Ten 00/100 Dollars, gold coin of the
United States of America, to them in hand paid by the said parties of the second part,
the receipt whereof is hereby acknowledged, do by these presents, grant, bargain and
sell, convey and confirm unto the said parties of the second part, and to their heirs
and assigns forever, all that certain real property, situate, lying and being in the
said County of San Luis Obispo, State of California, and bounded and particularly described as follows, to-wit:
Beginning at the South east corner of Section 19 in Township 27 South of Range 10
East Mount Diablo Meridian, and running thence North along the East line of said Section
440 yards to the North East corner of the South East quarter of the South East quarter
of said section; thence west 125 yards, more or less, to the public road leading from
Cambria to San Miguel; thence Westerly along the South line of said road following its
meanderings to the west line of the South East quarter of said Section; thence South
430 yards, more or less, to the South West corner of said South East quarter of said
Section; thence East half a mile to the place of beginning, containing 50 acres more
or less, and being a portion of the South half of the South East quarter of said
Section Nineteen (19); the North West quarter of Section Twenty-nine (29); the North
East quarter, the North half of the South East quarter, the South West quarter of the
South East quarter, the East half of the North West quarter, the East half of the South
West quarter and Lots one (1), two (2), three (3) and four (4) of Section thirty (30)
Lots one (1) and two (2) and the East one-half of the North West quarter and the North

Courtesy: Robert Soto
1910 Deed from Carpenter and Ivins to Ed Asebez and Cipriano Soto

As mentioned before, Cipriano Soto and Edward Asebez purchased the upper home ranch on August 8, 1910. This allowed Cipriano to move his family to the headwaters of Santa Rosa Creek in Cambria. Then on April 25, 1925, Ed and Louisa Asebez sold their half share to Andrew and Ernest Soto. Before this, Cipriano and his family lived in Cayucos. According to an August 5, 1965, oral interview of Lorin "Lowell" Thorndyke by Cambria historian Paul Squibb, Cipriano and his family lived in the house at 151 "C" Street in Cayucos. Thorndyke mentions that the Biagginni family owned this house and the shop next door in the old Wells Fargo Building. Cipriano operated a meat market for a short time out of this same shop. Cayucos, however, did not provide the upbringing Cipriano wished for his young children, and he desperately wanted to move his family back to the country.

Courtesy: Robert Soto

1925 Deed from Asebez to Ernest and Andrew Soto

In 1908, while living in Cayucos, young Ernest and Andrew became friends with an older crowd. In fact, as young boys, Ernest and Roy Genardini broke into the U.S. Post Office and robbed the money from the cashier's box. This was only a few dollars, but in those times (Ernest was about eight years old) money was very scarce. When the robbery became known, and because the Post Office was a federal facility, the Federal Bureau of Investigation (FBI) was brought in on the case. Fortunately, the FBI was looking for adults who burglarized this building and stole federal funds, not eight-year-old boys. In 1910, Cipriano purchased the upper ranch on Santa Rosa Creek and moved the boys out of town and back to the country. The robbery case remains unsolved to this day. Young Roy Genardini later became the Constable (sheriff) of Cayucos.

The Soto home ranch, lying at the headwaters of Santa Rosa Creek, comprised roughly 965 acres. Adjacent to the Soto Ranch and farther up the secluded canyon was the Roy Summers Ranch. Near the top of Santa Rosa Creek watershed, situated on Summers land, lay several immense rock formations that uniquely identify this property. These enormous boulders are visible from the north side of Highway 46 near the summit.

Cipriano told the story of a reclusive Captain Joseph Clark of San Simeon, a former whaler, who stayed in a small lean-to shed below these massive rocks. In retirement, Captain Clark became somewhat of a recluse living in his tiny shack, with only a corral for his horse and naturally formed rock cave to withstand the severe elements. Clark enjoyed this isolation and would come out of the mountains for supplies only once a month. Occasionally, Cipriano would deliver groceries on horseback to Clark's remote spot, since there was no road but only a narrow mountain trail leading to this secluded site. Interesting items have been discovered at this secret place, revealing insights into its past. Today, a hundred years later, nearly everything has vanished and the land has returned to its natural setting, revealing few clues of its fascinating history.

Although the story of San Simeon's Captain Clark has been passed down through the family, its accuracy is questionable since Captain Clark reputably died in 1891. The date of his death would be nearly twenty years before Cipriano moved to the upper ranch. Could Cipriano have been recalling another sea captain? Was there another Captain Clark? Whatever the case, the story remains with the Soto family and continues to be passed down through time.

While Cipriano and his wife, Carmel, owned this rough, mountainous ranch property, several other families struggled to make a living on this plot of land by working on shares, milking cows, farming, or cutting firewood.

On the westerly upper portion of the Soto home ranch identified as the "Timbers," at least three pioneer families lived in a little old house.

This area was appropriately named because it once was covered with many trees, which were cut for firewood to be used at Hearst Castle. After clearing this high flat, it became a farmable field for oat hay and even suitable for dairy cows.

Reno "Dad" Ingles and his wife, Lavina, were the first family to live at the Timbers. Dad Ingles built the Timbers barn and also the barn down the hill, near the present-day house of Jim Soto. Due to high winds in the mountains, both barns have fallen down, and the area has been cleared. It's believed these barns were built during the 1920s and 1930s.

Courtesy: Robert Soto
Barn "Dad" Ingles built at Home Ranch; circa 1970s

After the Ingles family, the Reis family lived at the Timbers and milked cows on shares. The milk was fed to the pigs, while the valuable cream was separated and hauled down the hill on horseback to a small wood collection stand for pickup every three days. Employees of the Harmony Valley Creamery Association traveled up all the local canyons to pick up cream and take it back to Harmony for processing and cheese making. The Reis family had four boys—Frank, Eddie, Joe, and Johnny—all of whom worked the land with their parents.

After the Reis family, the Lorin Thorndyke family was the last family to move into the Timbers and milk cows. Lorin was the son of Captain Thorndyke of the Piedras Blancas Lighthouse. Maud (Rogers) and Lorin Thorndyke also lived in this little house on the upper flat. Water was scarce and had to be pumped from a hand-dug well by a one-cylinder gasoline engine to a redwood water tank perched on an elevated wooden platform near the house and barn.

Down the canyon and adjacent to the Timbers, Lorin's brother and his wife, John Emory "Em" and Clara Erma (Rogers) Thorndyke, owned and operated another dairy at the present-day El Monte Ranch. Vernon and his first cousin Andrew Soto, Jr. ("Snow") occasionally helped Em milk his cows. It was considered a special treat to work for Em Thorndyke because Erma was widely known for being an excellent cook. Vernon recalls walking back to the house after milking to be treated to a special breakfast, including French toast, bacon, eggs, and so on. French toast was unheard of and a rare treat for the Soto boys.

Milking the cows was a life's work for the early pioneers. It required rising before the sun did, heading outside even on cold and wet mornings, only to milk again in the evening at dark. The facilities were poor; crude wooden stanchions locked the milk cow's heads while each was milked by hand. Sometimes, if facilities were very primitive, the cows would be milked outside in the elements. Often the old Swiss dairymen would strap a hand-carved oak wooden stool around their waist with one short center peg leg. This stool provided a brief rest and allowed the dairyman to sit while bending over during the exhausting milking job. Milking was extremely physical and demanding work, requiring powerful hand and arm strength. The remnants of a twelve-volt lighting system, which once illuminated the milking area, were discovered at the Timbers. At one time there were many lights attached to the barn and trees, allowing the industrious men to work during the dark early mornings and late nights.

In 1939, when Lorin Thorndyke tested his dairy cows for brucellosis, the results were devastating. Half of the cows tested positive and had to be destroyed. The following year, when the cows were tested again (tests were required for two consecutive years), half of the cows again tested positive. This huge loss proved to be "the straw that broke the camel's back." The Thorndyke family was forced to leave this beautiful high-mountain flat and move to Cayucos.

In 1955, Shirlene Soto, Cipriano's great granddaughter, remembered driving up to the old Timbers house with her grandmother Elsie to put out fresh meat to dry. Because the old house was warm, it served as an excellent place to dry venison jerky. There were no closable windows or doors on the abandoned house at this time, thus allowing for excellent air circulation.

Courtesy: Robert Soto

Cipriano, Andrew and Arthur Terrill on hay wagon at Home Ranch coming down from Timbers

Old window screens were used to keep flies and yellow jackets off the meat. However, Shirlene recalled that Elsie picked up several vicious meat-eating yellow jackets with her fingers and threw them away from the drying jerky. Elsie had no fear of these insects and was rarely stung.

The old Timbers house stood lonely and abandoned for sixty years. In 2004, the elements finally took their toll on this aged structure when it collapsed and was burned.

The San Simeon Story (1958), written by Margarita Griggs Smith, contains several great stories about Cipriano Soto, his brother Bernardino "Barney" Soto, Barney's wife, Margaret, and their relationship with the Hearst family. This book mentions the early history of San Simeon and includes this passage:

Old first-line California families, the Castros, Estradas, Sotos, watch silently from the shadows. So the Americans have come, so they bring with them gringo ways and gringo things, but no matter.

The short historical account describes how George and Phoebe Hearst never came to the ranch any more:

> The ranch house is now the permanent home of Virginian Captain Murray Taylor (the Hearst Ranch superintendent), his wife, his recently widowed daughter and his small grandson Mony [*sic*] Schutz.

Mr. Taylor was often remembered by Cipriano and always referred to as the "Virginian" because he came from that state. Taylor, the Virginian, used many Eastern expressions such as "Shaw." This phrase was heavily borrowed by Cipriano for the rest of his life. Cipriano was often heard saying to his wife Carmel, "Oh, Shaw, Misses."

When Mr. Taylor's governess announced her desire to get married, the Taylors realized a new replacement must be found immediately. It seems someone had a friend who had governess experience in Oregon, and she was desperate for a job:

> The newcomer is no bigger than a minute and she has a towering pompadour of red hair that seems top heavy for the parchment white face beneath it. This is the new governess? This tiny little English wisp?
>
> The dark, husky Hearst coachman [Cipriano Soto] meets her at the wharf and tells his brother [Bernardino], who is the head vaquero, all about it. To the coachman and the vaquero, members of a first-line Spanish California family, the little English Governess is an enigma. She'll be going back on the first steamer.

As a nine-year-old girl, Margaret's (who became the governess) first job earned her fifty cents a week. This job lasted twenty weeks, and she was paid with a ten-dollar gold piece. She recalled in her elder years the special feeling when that gold coin was placed in her hand. Margaret was a young woman when she started the job in San Simeon. Margaret came from a very poor family where she cooked, cleaned, washed, and ironed, taking care of her seven brothers and sisters while attending school. All this experience provided the background for Margaret's new job as governess.

The Smith book also contains this passage describing Margaret arriving in San Simeon by ship:

The tide had been so low that early May morning in 1900 that they couldn't put the gang plank out: so they'd tucked the little English senorita in a steamer chair, hoisted her up by a boom and swung her off onto the wharf. The coachman [Cipriano] had lifted the frightened, sick little thing into the coach. She'd been so scared and sick, he later told his brother [Barney], that she'd waved her hand toward the date painted on the warehouse and whispered weakly: 1878…that's the year I was born. If I die before I get to the house, that's the year that goes on my tombstone – 1878.

Couresty: Bill Strasen
Margaret (Ingles) Soto being lifted onto San Simeon pier; 1900

Margaret recalled her life at San Simeon:

She re-lives, for a moment, the wonderful shopping excursion they took to San Luis Obispo last month and the fabulous Ramona Hotel in which they stayed. What should she write about… the cattle drives to the goldtree station that took four days, of how men stopped at Green Valley for chicken dinner, of how those skinny, raw boned longhorns stampeded a lady's garden just outside of Morro Bay? Of the first time she climbed Red Rock (Morro Rock)? Of how she and the vaquero [Bernardino] carved their initials in a huge old oak tree up there? Dear Mother, she finally writes, I don't know what I'm in love with: the cowboy hat, the boots, or the vaquero himself.

Margaret Ingles married Bernardino Soto in 1902, and she later recalled in *The San Simeon Story:*

Family reunions out at her husband's old homestead. It takes three days to get there, though it is just over the crest of the Lucias. The trek is reminiscent of the ranchero days when two-wheeled carretas rattled between the ranches. The reunion is a month-long affair and her husband's "granpa", an old Castilian gent [General Soto] with a home-made peg-leg, makes the time fly with daily installments of the old ranchero days of San Simeon, when HE and his Castilian neighbors led the lives of Dons.

Courtesy: Karen (Soto) Snow
Soto family climbing over grade to visit Dry Bones Homestead; 1906

The San Simeon Story by Smith closes with a description of Margaret Soto in the 1956 Cambria Pinedorado Parade:

The crowd whistles and claps as Grand Marshall W.R. Hearst, Jr. rides by on his prized Arabian stallion and just behind him The Grand Old Lady, the little English governess [Margaret Ingles Soto] who stayed and became the bride, and later the widow, of the head Vaquero. With her black Spanish mantilla framing her pale English coloring, she is the symbol of San Simeon itself.

Margaret's brother, Reno "Dad" Ingles, also moved to the Cambria area and later had a daughter, Violet, who married Cipriano's elder son, Andrew.

All the Soto brothers worked as cowboys for the Hearst Ranch at various times in their lives. Bernardino Francisco "Barney" (often nicknamed "BF") Soto had a story written about him in the San Luis Obispo *Telegram-Tribune* by historian Dan Krieger. On July 16, 1906, the Hearst Ranch vaqueros were driving a herd of two hundred head of cattle from San Simeon to Goldtree (near today's California Men's Colony) to be loaded on the train. It took approximately three days to drive the cattle from San Simeon to San Luis Obispo and one day to head home. Somewhere west of today's Cuesta College, a Mr. Wallace drove his car into the herd. Barney Soto requested that the vehicle stop until the herd had passed, but Mr. Wallace paid no attention. The result was that the entire herd scattered and stampeded, making it very hard for the Hearst Ranch vaqueros. After several hours of gathering the cattle, the cattle drive reassembled. Later, the same car returned from Morro Bay heading towards San Luis Obispo and right into the herd again. Mr. Wallace was intoxicated and paid no heed to the warnings to stop. The vehicle actually struck one steer, breaking the car's headlight. Mr. Taylor, the cow boss of the Hearst Ranch, took out his lariat and roped a passenger in the vehicle to get the attention of the driver, Mr. Wallace. In these early days, the Highway Patrol or traffic laws did not exist. However, this situation did end up in court in San Luis Obispo and the driver was charged only with being drunk in public (because there were so few written driving laws at this time).

Barney and Margaret Soto lived in Cambria during their retirement years at a grand house adjacent to the present-day Brambles Restaurant on Burton Drive. Barney, Cipriano's younger brother, was born on June 11, 1879, in Jolon and died in Cambria on April 13, 1950. Margaret Rachel (Ingles) Soto died on November 7, 1958. Both Margaret and Barney are buried in the Cambria Catholic Cemetery.

Barney and Margaret Soto had two sons—Archie (1904-1978) and Edwin (1912-1986). Archie worked at the Hearst Ranch in San Simeon from the 1930s to 1951. His oral history in 1976 detailed his early life working at the Hearst Ranch. Archie thoroughly enjoyed his life as a cowboy:

> I liked to work on the ranch. It was a nice place to work. There was a lot of country. You would never ride in the same place twice. There was never a day without riding on horseback somewhere. That's what I liked and that's what I did. Then I got to be foreman, and that made it even better yet. I didn't have to go anywhere unless I wanted to.

Courtesy: Robert Soto
Barney Soto roping calves at Hearst Ranch

Archie's wife, Muriel, was a schoolteacher and taught at both the Santa Rosa School and Mammoth Rock School. They didn't have any children.

In the 1940s and 1950s, Edwin Soto raised cattle and milked cows in the family tradition near Villa Creek, north of Cayucos. Eventually Edwin moved his family to Cayucos, where in 1963 he purchased and operated the Cayucos Liquor Store. Edwin and Rita (Minetti) Soto had one daughter, Teresa "Terri" Soto. Terri retired from the Cambria branch of Bank of America in 2006. She carries the beautiful red hair inherited from her grandmother Margaret (Ingles) Soto.

Courtesy: Karen (Soto) Snow
Young "Pico" and Edwin Soto with Cambria School in background

In 1895, Cipriano and Carmel's honeymoon included a trip to San Francisco. This was a big event in their lives since it probably was the first trip to a big city for either of them. They rented a room in a downtown hotel. When it was time to retire, these true country folks tried unsuccessfully to blow out the lights (they were familiar with candles and kerosene lamps only). Cipriano went to the window that looked out over San Francisco and quickly saw a sea of lights glistening all over the city. Not being used to electricity, he looked over to his new bride and announced, "I guess these city folks sleep with the lights on!" On this special evening, the newlyweds went to bed and slept with all the room lights on. In 1895, electricity was a totally new concept to Cipriano and Carmel Soto.

When Cipriano purchased his first car, he was very excited about it. Carefully learning to drive and handle the new vehicle was a responsibility he took seriously. However, learning anything new can be overwhelming and, in critical situations, technical knowledge can easily be forgotten. That's exactly what happened to Cipriano when he brought his new car home and attempted to guide it into a narrow shed. When it was time to apply the brakes, all he could think to do was shout "Whoa!" But this failed to stop the car and it crashed into the front of the shed.

In 1940, Cipriano's elder son, Andrew, purchased a brand new Plymouth. He was very proud of this new vehicle and couldn't wait to show it off to his parents, Cipriano and Carmel. Andrew drove the new vehicle out to the Hearst San Simeon Ranch so everyone could inspect it. Cipriano and Carmel climbed into the front seat while young Jim (Andrew's younger son) viewed the vehicle from the back seat. After playing with the controls, the adults left and went into the ranch house, leaving young six-year-old Jim alone in the car. He soon noticed the cigarette lighter on the dashboard, pushed it in, and the knob turned red showing that it was hot. Jim then "branded" the new seats with the cigar lighter. The brands made a perfect circle. What fun! Andrew soon came out to check on his son and gave out a scream upon seeing the damage to the upholstery in his new car. Young Jim jumped out of the car and ran as fast as he could towards the outhouse. Andrew was fast on Jim's heels and, in anger, ripped off the door to the outhouse. Jim was about to receive his punishment, but Grandmother Carmel came to the rescue and saved young Jim from an embarrassing spanking.

Cipriano's left arm was badly broken as a young man from a horse accident. He didn't go to a doctor and, as a result, his arm was not set and didn't heal properly. He always extended his left arm out somewhat awkwardly, and he couldn't properly bend his elbow. Being right-handed, this never became a disability to him, for he simply adjusted his use of the injured arm. He was very agile and could easily mount any horse effortlessly.

Cipriano, like his brothers, was known as an excellent cowboy, horseman, athlete, and roper. While living on the Hearst Ranch at San Simeon Creek (today's Pedotti Ranch), he trained horses to sell for use in polo matches. These horses required an excellent light rein and were extremely well-trained by Cipriano. He would often enter reining competitions in the local rodeo events. Being extremely athletic, he entered several county-wide sporting events as a young man. His favorite event was the skip–hop–and–jump. This was similar to today's long jump event where speed, agility, and strength proved essential. Cipriano often won these local meets.

Another charming story about Cipriano and Carmel is when they were driving up the old Highway 1 coastline. Cipriano was reading signs aloud along the roadside as they zoomed by at speeds of twenty to thirty mph. Due to mountainous road conditions travel was slow and it was not unusual to see mudslides during the winter months. When Cipriano read

Courtesy: Karen (Soto) Snow
Carmel Soto in yard at Home Ranch with steep sidehill in background; circa 1920

"Slide Ahead" the next thing he noticed was Carmel, sitting down on the floorboards. He asked her, "Misses, what are you doing down there on the floor?" Carmel sheepishly looked up and responded to her husband, you told me to "slide ahead!"

Cipriano loved animals. Jim Soto recalled a special dog Cipriano once owned. It was a greyhound cross that was very smart, fast, and a fantastic hunter. The dog's name was "Pup." This dog could actually run down a coyote and destroy it; Pup, by himself, once even killed a dangerous badger, something extremely unusual. Pup could be vicious, and he seemed to enjoy a fight. Cipriano, while living near San Carpojo, was at a round-up one day when a friend told him to keep Pup away from his dog or his dog would kill Pup. Tired of his friend boasting about his dog, Cipriano said nothing. But at an opportune time, he quietly looked at Pup and whispered, "Sic him." Pup lunged at the other dog and quickly got the best of him. The owner began shouting, "Call off Pup before he kills my dog!" This secretly brought a smile to Cipriano's face.

Before the availability of television and radio, the Soto family often told ghost stories in the evenings. Cipriano and Carmel both loved to tell these stories, and great care would go into every detail. Usually everyone was so scared that they had trouble sleeping at night. One evening when Cipriano was riding through the mountains on his way home, he rode under an oak tree. Unbeknownst to him, a small branch broke off and lodged in his jacket collar. As he was riding, he would occasionally catch a glimpse of something following him over his shoulder. Remembering all the ghost stories, he began to ride harder and faster on his way home. However, no matter how fast he went, the shadow was always right behind him. Were the ghost stories finally coming true? Reaching home at dusk, he quickly unsaddled and hurried into the house to tell the "Misses" about his episode. As he was explaining his story, Carmel reached behind his collar and pulled out the branch. They both quickly realized that the branch was the mysterious "shadow" following him through the hills and got a good laugh.

Carmel would often speak of the cucasues ("coo-ca-sue-es"). This was a Spanish slang word for ghosts or the boogieman—the cucasues are going to get you if you don't do such and such. Carol (Soto) Lowry vividly remembered as a little girl listening to Grandma Carmel's bedtime scary stories. When Carmel was near the end of her story she would raise the bedcovers and shake them, saying "Be careful or the cucasues will get

Courtesy: Steven Soto
Cipriano Soto riding horseback in early Cambria Parade; circa 1940s

you!" It's unknown where it originated, but fifty years after Carmel died in 1964, this scary word continues to bring shivers down my spine.

Cipriano was an extremely kind and respectful person and took great care of his wife. He brought her coffee in bed every morning. Making coffee was not the simple task it is today because this was before electric coffee makers. Cipriano would get up early and build a wood fire in the kitchen stove. He would carefully slice small kindling and place it over paper, sprinkle on a small amount of kerosene and light the fire. One early morning he grabbed the wrong fuel can and poured white gas (used for lanterns) on the fire instead of kerosene. Jim Soto recalled being awakened by a huge explosion in the kitchen. When he ran into the room, the round steel stove plates had dented the kitchen ceiling, and Cipriano was standing there without eyebrows or eyelashes and with a scorched mustache. Jim recalled hearing a few words that were new to him.

Cipriano was honored by being included in Byron Hanchett's book, *In and Around the Castle* (1985). A chapter is devoted to Cipriano as a western gentleman. As he matured, he dressed western, not as a cowboy, but as a western gentleman. In this book, Cipriano describes being coachman for Phoebe Apperson Hearst and driving the Studebaker carriage. A large photo of him is included with the article and the caption states:

Courtesy: Robert Soto
Cipriano Soto, Grand Marshall of SLO La Fiesta de las Flores Parade; 1948

Fiesta Grand Marshal… Cipriano Soto 78, San Simeon, born at the old San Antonio Mission on Mexican Independence day, Sept 16, 1870, is grand marshal of the 20th Annual Fiesta de las Flores parade Saturday morning. He will be riding a handsome stallion from the famed Hearst Ranch, bedecked in the silver trappings for which the Hearst stable is world famed. Soto has worked for the Hearst ranch since he was 17 years old. He was coachman for Mrs. Phoebe Hearst, mother of William Randolph Hearst, taking her to and from San Simeon and San Luis Obispo many times in coach and four.

Doris Ingles (a man, whose sister married Andrew Soto) shared an account of a childhood incident during his stay with Augustine "Gus" Soto at Jolon (on the Hearst Ranch) near Mission San Antonio. Every year Gus and his family would plant corn in the spring to have food for the late summer months. Doris Ingles stayed with Gus's family one spring when it was time to plant the corn. Gus worked the ground with his team of horses and heavy plow until it was just right to plant. The family asked young Doris if he would like to be responsible for planting the corn that year. Doris was proud to have this responsibility and willingly accepted the offer. After loading the corn seed in the planter and working hard to get the rows straight and just right, Doris was soon ready to go home to his family. Disappointingly, he never got to see his seeds sprout. After two weeks Gus questioned his wife as to why the corn wasn't coming up, but they decided to wait a little longer. Week after week went by and still no corn sprouted until finally it was too late to plant again. No one could understand why the seed didn't sprout until Gus finally looked in the corn planter and discovered the corn seeds still in the hopper. Young Doris had failed to open the planter's small door, allowing the seed to drop to the ground. That year there was no corn for the Soto family.

The Terrill family was an integral part of the Soto family. Newell E. Terrill married Josefa Asebez (Carmel's oldest sister) in 1892. Newell's family came from the Adelaida area and moved to San Simeon, where young Newell worked as a bartender at the Bayview Hotel (near present-day Sebastian's Store). Newell died at a very early age from pneumonia, leaving his young wife, Josefa, and two sons, Arthur and Edward Terrill. At the young age of thirty-two, Josefa died, leaving the two young boys without either parent. Young Eddie Terrill moved in with his uncle, Edward Asebez, and wife Louisa (Soto) Asebez. Arthur Terrill lived at the home ranch with Cipriano and his Aunt Carmel until he went into the army.

Courtesy: Karen (Soto) Snow
Don "Pancho" Estrada with Augustine "Gus" Soto, San Simeon Beach

Family friend Francis Rademacker recounted Cipriano telling a story about Ernest Soto and Arthur Terrill when they were young men. There was always work to accomplish on the ranch and never enough time to socialize. Since these young men were close in age, they discovered girls about the same time. The opportunity to meet young women when working on the ranch was very limited, but just over the hill to the west was the Bassi Ranch in Green Valley. Mr. Bassi had three daughters (Mary, Sylvia, and Olivia), and the Sotos would ride over to visit occasionally. One day it was getting late and the cows hadn't been milked. Cipriano couldn't find the boys and discovered through Andrew that both Arthur and Ernest had gone "courting." Cipriano was upset because the cows had not been milked and the "Misses" was worried about the boys. Andrew and Cipriano went to saddle their horses to ride over to Bassi's Ranch, but there was no saddle for Andrew because the boys had used two saddles. This required Andrew to use the workhorse with its harness and blinders, while Cipriano rode a colt he was breaking for the Bassis. It was about 8:30 p.m. when they left on that Sunday evening. Because it was wintertime, the ground was soft and slippery for the horses. Making their way through the mountainous terrain in the dark added some danger to the ride. Once outside the Bassi's Green Valley home, Cipriano peeked through a window where he could see the two boys playing cards with the Bassi girls. Desperately trying to control his temper, Cipriano went to the front door and knocked. Mr. Bassi opened the door and said, "Hello, Mr. Soto." Cipriano calmly responded, "Hello, Mr. Bassi, would you please send my boys outside? Thank you very much." The boys came out of the house like whipped pups, as Cipriano sternly reminded them that they had chores to complete before they could socialize. The boys sheepishly climbed on their horses and headed back over the hill with Cipriano and Andrew. Not one word was uttered all the way home. It was a long ride back to the Soto Ranch. Arthur Terrill would later marry Olivia Bassi and have two children, Obie and Newell.

Courtesy: Robert Soto

**Obie and Newell Terrill, Vernon and Snow Soto
on San Simeon house porch with Cipriano; circa 1929**

Ed and Helen Evans were neighbors and very good friends of Cipriano and Carmel when they lived up the coast at San Carpojo on the Hearst Ranch. The Evans family was very active and lived life to the fullest. They were constant pranksters and really enjoyed a good joke. The Soto family often told the story of Ed Evans and his wife inviting Cipriano and Carmel over for supper. Cipriano drove his little car up the coast road to the entrance of the Evans Ranch. Pausing to get out of the vehicle and open the gate, he didn't realize that Ed was hiding behind a bush near the gate. Ed was quite pleased with himself because he had nailed the gate shut, making it impossible for Cipriano to open it. After several minutes of frustration trying to open the difficult gate, Ed jumped out from behind the bush and shouted, "Hey Soup!" (Cipriano was often called "Soup" or "The Boss"). The boss's nickname did not refer to Cipriano as being bossy but rather as someone who was in charge. Carmel's nickname was always "The Misses."

Ed Evans played another trick on Cipriano and Carmel when they were getting ready for supper at the Evans's house. Ed had a large pile of wood outside in the yard that needed to be split. Cipriano noticed this, and it became a topic of conversation before dinner. When they began discussing the woodpile, Ed noticed out of the corner of his eye, a hobo walking up the lane towards the house. (It wasn't unusual in these days to have hobos or tramps come around and work for food.) Upon seeing the hobo approaching his door, Ed looked up to heaven and began praying out loud, "Lord please bring me someone to split this wood for me!" Cipriano was startled by Ed's outburst because he was not one to pray out loud. Then as soon as Ed finished his prayer, a knock came at the front door. Ed shouted, "My prayers have been answered!" Everyone got a good laugh out of this. The wood was split and the hobo got supper.

Cipriano smoked a corncob pipe when he was an older man. Ed Evans used this knowledge to play another prank on him. Unnoticed by Cipriano, Ed carefully loaded Cipriano's pipe with a small plug of gunpowder. When Cipriano lit his trusty pipe and the flame burned down to the gunpowder, it went "POW!" Cipriano surely knew immediately who was responsible for this.

In May 1945, newly married Vernon and Althea Soto hosted a large golden wedding anniversary party for Cipriano and Carmel. Vernon and Althea were living at the historic Taylor house in Green Valley while they milked cows on shares. Newlywed Althea recalled her mother-in-law, Elsie, bringing all the food and organizing this special event. Elsie wanted the party to be held in Green Valley, where there was more space available, better parking, and easier access than up at the ranch house where she was living on the Summers's place. This was a very special event attended by many family members. The local newspaper printed the following article.

MR. AND MRS. CIPRIANO SOTO HONORED ON GOLDEN WEDDING

The golden wedding anniversary of Mr. and Mrs. Cipriano Soto was the occasion for the gathering of a large group of relatives at the home of Mr. and Mrs. Vernon Soto and Andrew Soto Jr., in Green Valley last Sunday. At 12:30 the guests enjoyed a delicious barbecue followed by an afternoon of visiting.

Mrs. Soto was born in Cambria and Mr. Soto was born and raised in the Jolon country. Later he went to work on the Hearst ranch as a coachman, where he met Miss Carmel Asabez, and they were married in the Old Mission in San Luis Obispo. They made their home in San Simeon for a few years where their three children, Andrew, Ernest and Evelyn were born, and then moved to Cambria where Mr. Soto worked as a butcher for Mora, Hitchcock, Asabez and Ford. He later worked for the same people in Cayuos for a while. They then moved to the Ivans place on upper Santa Roza creek where they lived for a number of years. Their home now is on a ranch near San Carpojo creek.

* * *

The following attended the celebration: Mr. and Mrs. J. M. Soto, Mr. and Mrs. B. F. Soto, Mr. and Mrs. Edwin Soto, Mr. and Mrs. Archie Soto, Mr. and Mrs. J. A. Soto, Mr. and Mrs. Gus Soto, Mr. and Mrs Andrew Soto, Mr. and Mrs. M. Barba, Mr. and Mrs. Laurence Mora and family, Mr. and Mrs. R. A. Mora, Mr. and Mrs. Glen Thompson and family, Mr. and Mrs. Ed Garcia, Mr. and Mrs. Edward Asabez, Mr. and Mrs. Arthur Terril, Mr. and Mrs. Vernon Soto, Mr. and Mrs. Ernest Soto, Mr. and Mrs. L. R. Ingles, Mrs. Sybil White, Miss Betty Soto, Raymond Asabez, Oliver Terrill, Lee Gunther, Miss Carol Soto, Miss Evelyn Soto, James Bianchini, Edmond Barlogio, Andrew Soto Jr., and Jimmy Soto.

Courtesy: Karen (Soto) Snow

Newspaper article of Cipriano and Carmel's 50th Wedding Anniversary; May 1945

Courtesy: Robert Soto
Cipriano and Carmel Soto's 50th Wedding Party, Green Valley; 1945

(From back left, standing) Vernon and Althea Soto, Betty Soto, Louisa Soto, James Bianchini, Laurence Mora, Andrew "Snow" Soto, Howard Williams, Edmondo Barlogio, Carol Soto, Raymond Asabez

(From left, back row sitting at table) Sybil White (Levina Ingles' sister), Levina Ingles, Ed Garcia, Cora Garcia,?,?, Evelyn Soto, Lilly Soto, Gus Soto, (standing at end of table) Cipriano Soto, Carmel Soto

(From left, front row) Edwin Soto, Rita Soto, Muriel Soto, Archie Soto, Lucylle Soto, Barney Soto, Lilly Mora, Rafael Mora

Rafael Mora

Rafael Mora was a half brother to Carmel's mother, Placida (Garcia) Asebez. The Mora family were neighboring ranchers with the Sotos for many years in upper Santa Rosa Creek and always considered close friends. In 1895, Rafael Mora and his wife, Josie Cantua, purchased the present-day Brambles property in downtown Cambria. The Moras lived in the Brambles house with their five sons and two daughters until 1908. At this point they moved up Santa Rosa Creek, where Mora built a slaughterhouse to supply his butcher shop in Cambria. Family stories recall Cipriano helping "Uncle Rafael" drive a herd of cattle through the hills of upper Santa Rosa Creek canyon and down into Cambria to the slaughterhouse. In 1915, the Moras moved back into the Cambria house, which had been empty, and the butcher shop was sold to his nephew, Edward Asabez. Asabez bought out partners Hitchcock and Mora and then took in a new partner, Joaquin "Jack" Soto.

Jack Soto went to work as a butcher for his brother-in-law, Edward Asabez, and also for Ed Hitchcock, who operated the Rocky Butte Cattle Company. This early training would lead Jack into starting his own butcher shop and grocery store in 1917. The Soto family and friends always called Jack by the nickname "The Butcher."

Courtesy: Karen (Soto) Snow
Lila Soto with Soto's Market delivery truck; 1936

Vernon Soto recalls Jack Soto having a small slaughtering plant in Cambria. This plant was in a drainage ditch below the present-day middle school, adjacent to Main Street. At this site cattle were shot, hanged, skinned, quartered, and then taken down to Soto's Market. Ernest Soto often sold cattle to Jack for processing at this small slaughter house. These were days long before grain feeding—all the cattle slaughtered were grass-fed.

In 1910, Jack Soto married Agnes "Aggie" Maggetti at Mission San Luis Obispo. The day before the wedding, chaperones Barney and Margaret Soto took them on the day-long carriage ride into San Luis Obispo. They

Courtesy: Karen (Soto) Snow
Margaret "Dolly" and Joaquin Jr. "Pico" Soto

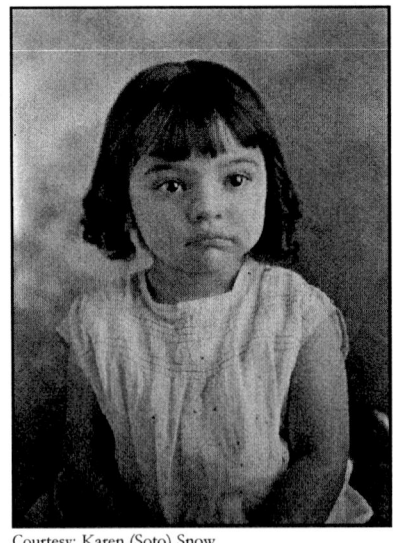

Courtesy: Karen (Soto) Snow
Youngest daughter, Betty (Soto) Williams; 1930

all spent the night in San Luis on the evening before the wedding. However, the next morning the newlyweds discovered that scheduling was a problem since Jack and Aggie had failed to ask for approval from the Cambria Catholic Church for their wedding. Because of this, the marriage took place at the odd time of six o'clock in the morning. On returning to Cambria, the Native Sons and Daughters held a huge "shivaree" in their honor. A shivaree was common for the time as a way to celebrate any special occasion.

Jack and Aggie had four children—Margaret "Dolly" (1911-2007), Joaquin, Jr. "Pico" (1913-1987), Lila (1915-2000), and Betty (b. 1925).

Edward Frank "Ponch" Asabez recalled a story about Jack Soto early in World War II and recorded his memories on tape. It seems that Ponch came to visit Jack and Aggie Soto for a barbecue one evening when, for entertainment, they listened to the radio. There was a great deal of false information at this time because of communication problems and the uncertainty of the war. There also was great fear that the Japanese would bomb the West Coast of California. Panic swept over everyone as the radio commentator announced that the Japanese were currently bombing the city of San Francisco. This was a great worry to Jack and Aggie because two of their girls, Dolly and Lila, were in the military and stationed in San Francisco. Since Jack and Aggie didn't have a telephone in their house, Jack decided to drive up to the grocery store to call his "girls" and see if they were all right. A call was quickly placed but with poor connections they had to wait until the girls could call back.

In the meantime, Jack pulled out a whiskey bottle from behind the store shelf and shared it with Ponch. This was a time of great concern, and the whiskey seemed to help smooth things over. After about an hour of drinking the phone finally rang and Dolly told her father that they were both fine and that the bombing was simply another false alarm. This brought enormous relief to both Jack and Ponch, so they decided to go next door and have a celebratory drink at Joe Reali's saloon. After a few rounds of drinks, it was getting very late and Jack went back to the meat market and selected some steaks and French bread so they could have a big celebration barbecue the next day. They drove back home, but first decided to "kill" the rest of the liquor bottle in the car before going inside to see Aggie. As they got out of the car and began walking up to the front door (perhaps staggering is a more accurate word), Jack dropped the French bread in the yard but was unable to pick it up. He told Ponch they would get the bread tomorrow. Finally, after a good night's sleep they awoke and began looking all over the house for the missing bread. Eventually going outside, they found the swollen bread "floating" in a puddle of water from recent rains; both men had a good laugh.

118 AN OLD CALIFORNIA FAMILY: THE SOTOS OF CAMBRIA

Courtesy: Steven Soto

Soto family picnic in Cayucos; early 1940s

From left: Archie Soto, Snow Soto, Margaret (Ingles) Soto, Jack Soto (guitar), Cipriano Soto, Barney Soto, Lilly (Messic) Soto, Carmel (Asebez) Soto, Evelyn Soto, Doris Ingles, Rita (Minetti) Soto, Levina Ingles, Muriel (Gillespie) Soto, Gus Soto, Aggie (Maggetti) Soto, Elsie (Barlogio) Soto, Ernest Soto, Jim Bianchini ("The Spider"), Andrew Soto, Lemuel Reno "Dad" Ingles (Edwin Soto took the photo)

The children of Cipriano and Carmel (Asebez) Soto were:

1. Andrew Asabez Soto   b. 1896   d. 1973
   m. 1923 Lorena Violet Ingles   b. 1903   d. 1938
   m. 1942 Lucylle Wagner   b. 1913   d. 2000
2. **Ernest Cipriano Soto**   **b. 1899   d. 1979**
   m. 1923 Elsie Letticia Barlogio   b. 1905   d. 1989
3. Evelyn Carmel Soto   b. 1900   d. 1995
   (Never married)

APPENDIX VIII

Edwin Terrill's Accident

Cipriano's youngest sister, Louisa "Beva" Soto (1890-1969), lived in Paso Robles during her later years. In 1910, Beva's first marriage was to Ed Asabez, the brother of Carmel (Asabez) Soto. A tragic event occurred on October 28, 1915, at the home of Beva and Ed Asabez. The following is from the daily *Telegram Tribune* newspaper, San Luis Obispo:

> A distressing affair occurred at Paso Robles between the hours of 12:00 and 1:00 a.m. yesterday morning. As a result of a mistake, Ed Asebez, a highly respected resident of that city shot and killed his nephew, Edwin N. Terrill, who he suspected was attempting to enter his home.
>
> Two or three of the young men about town, who had been carousing at a house near the Salinas River, are believed to have been the cause of the sad affair, according to reports received here yesterday.
>
> Mr. Asebez and his nephew had been spending the evening at the butcher shop owned by Messrs. Asebez, Hitchcock & Bagley, as had been their custom in straightening up the accounts of the day. At 10:00 p.m. they returned to the Asebez home in Park Street, and Mr. Asebez retired to his room while Terrill proceeded to his quarters which were in the basement of the house. Between the hours of 11:00 and 12:00 o'clock Mr. Asebez was aroused by his wife who told him there were intruders on the premises and that someone was attempting to gain entrance to the house. Mr. Asebez being slightly deaf could not discern the noises from outside of the house but his wife continued to hear them and a few moments afterward a man's voice was heard calling "John." Mrs. Asebez called out that there was no such person about the premises and for the intruder to leave. The occupants of the house are certain there were two men that were threatening to gain entrance as one of them was heard to say they would get into the house. Mrs. Soto [Dolores Grahalva Soto], mother of Mrs. Asebez [Louisa Soto Asebez], also heard the noise of the men outside and she and her daughter were becoming terrorized owing to the threats made by those on the outside, and the women cried out for help. In the meantime Mr. Asebez had gone to a closet and secured his rifle. He wished to summon his nephew from the basement and began pounding with the butt of the weapon on the floor in order that the noise would arouse him. Fearing

that the intruders outside would attempt to enter by way of the kitchen door, which had no lock, he went and placed a chair against it. Looking out of the front window a moment later he saw one man start to go around the back of the house, at the same time he heard the back door being forced open and peering through a pass-closet between the dining room he dimly saw the form of a man force his way through the door and started across the room as if to enter the room of Mrs. Soto. The supposed intruder was apparently trying to get his coat on as it was partly over his head and in the darkness Asebez, believing bodily harm would come to him and members of his family, fired a shot from his rifle through the opening of the pass-closet, the bullet entering the heart of the man opposite, who was instantly killed.

Turning on the lights Mrs. Soto exclaimed, 'Oh, Ed, you have killed Eddie.' It developed that when Terrill had heard the alarm above his room that he had dressed and had all his clothes on with the exception of his coat, which he was trying to get on in his haste to get into the house to answer the call for assistance.

Mrs. Asebez has been very ill for the past two weeks, and the affair, it is feared, will affect her condition. Mr. Asebez is greatly grieved as are also other members of his family. On the death of Terrill's mother, a few years ago, Asebez became the boy's protector and had proved a good guardian.

After the shooting Coroner Palmer of this city was notified, and immediately started for Paso Robles, accompanied by District attorney Palmer, Sheriff Taylor and Court Reporter Green. After investigating the circumstances the coroner's jury immediately rendered the following verdict:

"'That Edward N. Terrill, a native of California, age 22 years, came to his death by gunshot wound inflicted by one Ed Asebez. We further find deceased was mistaken for a housebreaker and that no blame is attached to said Asebez or to the deceased'."

The body will be brought to this city today and Thursday morning will be taken by motor funeral car to Cambria where the funeral will be held at 11 o'clock.

Terrill was born and raised in Cambria and had only gone to Paso Robles within the past few months where he was in the employ of his uncle and his partners in the meat market. Asebez had resided for years in Cambria before going to Paso Robles. The parties owing to their long distance in the county, had many friends who will regret to learn of such an unfortunate circumstance, which could not have been avoided under the circumstance, but it seems a pity that the persons who caused the disturbance outside the Asebez home, which led to such a distressing affair, can not be prosecuted.

APPENDIX IX

Jack Soto

Joaquin Modesto Soto, child number six in this large family, the youngest brother to Cipriano Soto, was commonly known as "Jack." He opened Soto's Market in 1917 in downtown Cambria and operated this business for many years. In fact, this specialty market continues to operate today with new owners. I wrote the following article for *The Cambrian* on July 10, 1997, about Jack Soto and his early life at Dry Bones.

Courtesy: Karen (Soto) Snow
**Joaquin "Jack" Soto, Grand Marshall of
SLO La Fiesta de las Flores; 1951**

Courtesy: Robert Soto

Jack's wife, Agnes (Maggetti) Soto, making tortillas

"Dry Bones"

by
Robert Soto

Some of the early pioneers in our area included the family of General Arculano Soto and his wife, Dolores Grahalva. It was this early day family who homesteaded 160 rugged acres near present-day Adelaida. Seven children were soon raised from this hardy stock to include the youngest son, Joaquin Modesto Soto, more commonly known as "Jack."

Life was extremely difficult for this family as they attempted to make their new start in a very barren and harsh environment. One of their first tasks was construction of a simple adobe structure, which would become home. As you can imagine, the family ranch did not earn the name "Dry Bones" from an easy beginning.

As with all ranching families, the children were also required to do their share of the chores. Times were not easy for young Jack, as being the youngest, he often inherited the least favorite jobs around the ranch. However, now it was time for young Jack to enter into manhood and accept some of the required responsibilities. His father, General, decided Jack was now old enough to take the team of horses into Paso Robles for the rare task of purchasing groceries.

It was not often these long and difficult trips were required. Money was very scarce in the early 1900s but the supplies were necessary for simple survival. This would finally be young Jack's opportunity to show his family he was indeed a responsible young man. Money was given to Jack with explicit instructions on exactly what was needed. There was no money for anything but the bare essentials.

Young Jack hitched up the team of horses and headed off alone in the buckboard to Paso Robles for the arduous two-day trip. Upon safe arrival it must have been a comfort to Jack to finally be on his own. That evening, with little else to do, Jack believed it surely wouldn't hurt to look in on the local poker game. After studying the game for awhile, young Jack was confident he could make some very easy money by just playing a few quick hands. There had to be an easier way to make money than the hard ranch life.

Young Jack would learn a lesson he would never forget on that evening. The local cardsharps soon took all the family money intended for groceries. Jack spent a long sleepless night thinking over every hand of that evening's game. The next morning after much deliberation, he decided to visit the grocer and ask about a loan for the necessary food staples. The grocer, knowing the Soto family well, decided young Jack was a good risk and allowed the credit.

The trip back to "Dry Bones" must have been especially long as Jack had plenty of time to lament on the past day's events. Imagine the thoughts passing through young Jack's mind as the slow buckboard meandered through the mountains towards Adelaida.

As Jack neared home he became very fearful of what his father would say. How could he explain his card-playing and losing all the family grocery money? As Jack stopped to open a gate along the path and got out of the wagon, he absent-mindedly forgot to tie the reins properly. Upon opening the gate, the horses "spooked" and bolted down the road towards home. Young Jack chased after the run-away wagon on foot but was unable to catch up for some distance. As Jack ran down the bumpy path he passed sacks of flour and dry staples scattered along the roadway. What else could possibly go wrong? This surely had to be a difficult lesson for a 15-year-old boy.

After picking up the scattered supplies, the determined Jack finally made it home. He now realized it was time to face his father and attempt to explain his way out of the situation. But first Jack's mother, Dolores, came to his rescue. Jack was severely scolded by his mother as he explained what happened. And as mothers often do, she also decided to "save" her youngest son. His mother had money stashed away from selling eggs that no one knew of. It was this money that would be used to repay the kind grocer in Paso Robles and get Jack out of trouble. General never learned of this episode with Jack and his gambling. I seriously doubt he would have been very sympathetic. Would you as a parent?

Young Jack finally grew up and moved with the rest of the Soto family to Cambria. In 1917, he established Soto's Market in downtown Cambria. I guess this early story of groceries stayed with Jack as he continued in the business for the rest of his life. However, Jack was always remembered as a kind gentleman who helped many families in difficult situations. Jack's daughters, Margaret and Lila Soto and Betty (Soto) Williams, all can recall many acts of kindness Jack bestowed on local families.

Dry Bones ranch was sold in 1971 by the Soto family to the Camp Fire Girls Council and renamed Camp Natoma. Jack must have thought back on his childhood days in Dry Bones and this traumatic situation. However, Jack never lost his love of poker as he played cards until his death in 1981.

GENERATION 6 (ERNEST)

Courtesy: Robert Soto
Young Ernest Soto on horseback at Summers Ranch; circa 1930s

Ernest Soto, middle child of Cipriano and Carmel, was born on the Hearst Ranch in San Simeon in 1899. Ernest and his wife, Elsie Letticia Barlogio, had only one child, Vernon Ernest Soto, born October 17, 1925.

Ernest's early memories as a young boy were of growing up on the Soto Ranch. He started grammar school while living in Cayucos and later completed his schooling when he graduated from eighth grade at the one-room Mammoth Rock School on Cambria's upper Santa Rosa Creek. When asked about attending high school in an oral interview by his granddaughter, Shirlene Soto, he said:

> No, I never heard of anything as a high school when I graduated. I went through eighth grade; I got my diploma for grammar school, but when I got my diploma for grammar school I never heard anybody say anything about the high school. Never knew about it, never went. I was through with school. You know, where there was no [outside influences], there was no activity, no news of any kind, and like the high school, you see, we never, you never heard of it. Never missed it because we never had it.

Recalling religion as a youth, Ernest said:

> We went to church once in awhile, very seldom, but my folks were all pretty religious, but we never went to church very much. 'Cause we couldn't get there. We had to go with the horses and it was a long ways, so we just never made a practice of that, but they were still very religious and did a lot of praying.

When asked about how his parents raised the three children, Ernest replied:

> There was nothing to be strict about. We were out in the country. You couldn't get into any mischief because there was no mischief in that whole area you know.

At thirteen, Ernest began his first job of milking cows for the Thorndyke neighbors. He earned $15 a month. Because Ernest grew up on the ranch, it seemed only natural that he would continue his life as a rancher. Ernest was a partner in the cattle operation with his older brother, Andrew. These two brothers were extremely close and had an unusual family relationship. Andrew lived on the home ranch, while Ernest lived in the rented house on the adjoining "Roy Summers" ranch. They kept a ranch checkbook together, and all business as well as personal matters went through this account. Their relationship was so close that if either Andrew or Ernest needed a new stove or refrigerator for his own house, it would be purchased out of the joint checkbook. This never created any questions or problems for either brother. The bond between these two brothers was so strong that often after spending the entire day working together, they would each go home for supper, only to call the other on the telephone and "visit" a little longer.

Ernest's nickname was "The Hound" while his brother, Andrew, was called "Deak." This nickname was short for "Deacon," a name given to Andrew because he was constantly preaching. Andrew often gave advice to his children and others on the right way to handle life's situations.

In the 1930s, Ernest and his brother, Andrew, hired workers to cut wood for the many fireplaces at Hearst Castle. This wood was cut from the upper Soto Ranch at places that we today call the "Timbers" and "Maccachi Camp." Before power chainsaws, this highly laborious task was extremely physical because everything had to be completed by hand. All wood had to be cut in four-foot lengths for the huge fireplaces at the Castle. Not only was the wood cut on the Soto Ranch but it also had to be delivered to the hilltop at San Simeon. I recently discovered an internal letter dated November 9, 1933, from the Hearst Hilltop Department, requesting payment for thirty-five cords of wood delivered to the hilltop from the Soto Brothers at $10 a cord. The letter states that the Sotos were poor and greatly needed their money. Imagine hauling wood up the steep Hearst Castle road using the old unreliable trucks Ernest and Andrew had. There's one story that Verl "Giggs" Ingles (brother of Violet Ingles Soto) was driving a load of firewood along Highway 1, near today's San Simeon Acres, when the truck's wheel flew off and rolled down into the ocean surf. The wheel and tire were retrieved from the pounding surf, re-installed, and Giggs continued with his delivery to the hilltop of Hearst Castle.

During the 1930s Depression, Ernest and Elsie were financially forced to move into San Luis Obispo so Ernest could work on the county road crew. His wages were essential for paying the property tax on the upper ranch. During this financially difficult time, many ranchers lost their land

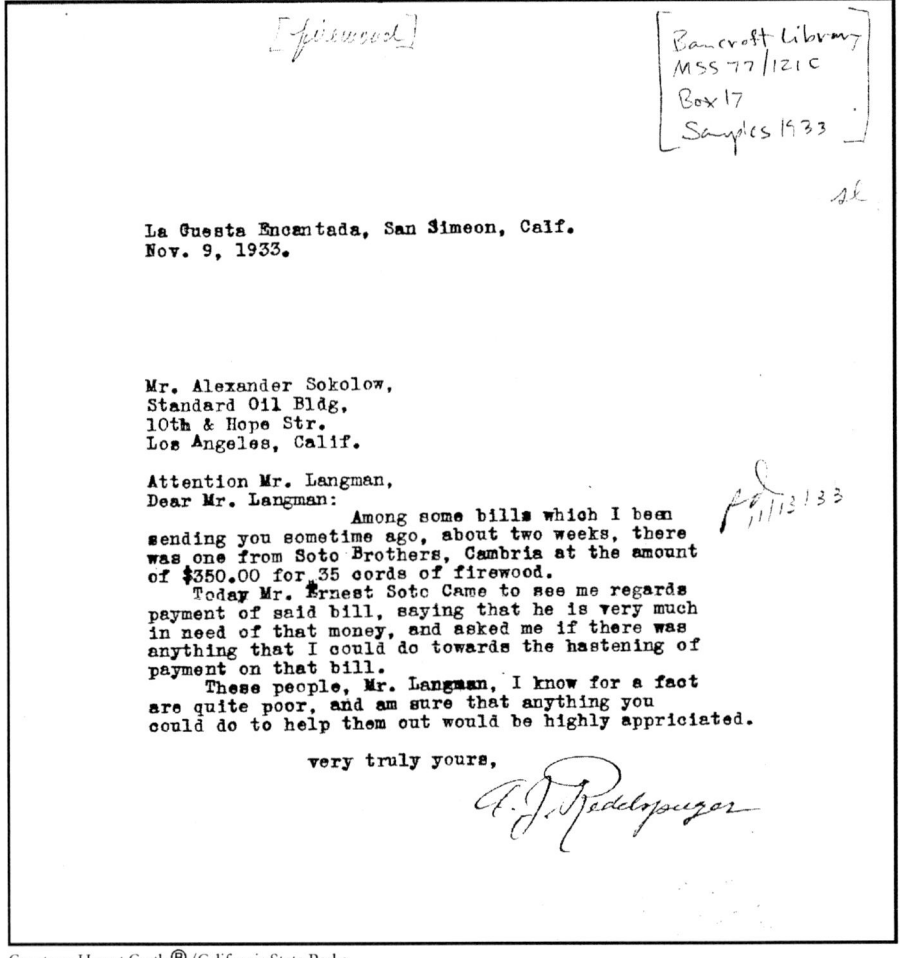

Courtesy: Hearst Castle®/California State Parks
Letter (Hearst Castle File) regarding payment to Soto Brother's for firewood

because property taxes could not be paid. Ernest held this county job for a few years until the family was able to move back to the Summers house on upper Santa Rosa Creek. Elsie's parents, James and Angelica Barlogio, lived in San Luis Obispo and financially assisted the young Soto family during these difficult times. Because of the move to San Luis, their son, Vernon, went to first and second grade in San Luis Obispo.

In 1935, as a young man, Ernest suffered physically from a very serious horse accident. Louis Fiscalini remembers breaking horses for both Andrew and Ernest. One particular horse was working extremely well, although he was known to be very high-spirited. Louis told Ernest that the horse was finally ready for him to take. Ernest was busy, however, with other projects around the ranch and wasn't able to ride this young horse for a few weeks. In haste, when Ernest finally found time to ride this fancy young gelding, he unfortunately did not warm up the horse properly. Ernest went down the road at a gallop and slid the horse to a stop. When he spun the horse around, it ducked its head and began bucking. Ernest tried to pull the horse's head up, but the young horse went straight over backwards with Ernest still aboard. Tragedy stuck as the saddle horn was jammed into his pelvis, fracturing and splitting it. He remained bed-ridden and in traction for three months. The horse was sold.

Courtesy: Karen (Soto) Snow
Young Archie and Ernest Soto all "dressed up" in early 1920s

Ernest began working on the San Simeon hilltop as a night watchman when Hearst Castle was transferred to the State of California in 1958. At the Castle, Ernest worked after dark into the early morning hours so that his own ranch work could also be completed during daylight hours. Security at Hearst Castle has always been considered very important. Later, Ernest worked in the grounds section under Supervisor Norman Rotanzi. Norman became a long-term fixture at the Castle, working on the hilltop for nearly sixty years. These outside jobs were necessary so that Ernest could make extra money during the difficult times of ranching.

Ernest never knew a stranger, for he was very outgoing and easy to talk to. He typically wore his Levi pants with the cuffs rolled up about two to three inches. Another unique trait was his short-brimmed felt hat that he wore in his elder years; this was much different from the typical cowboy hat.

Joe Botts, a neighbor from the Adelaida area, told a great story about Ernest. It was wintertime and Jack Botts (Joe's father, born in 1892) and his brother rode horseback over the Adelaida hills down into Santa Rosa Creek Valley to catch a steelhead. (This was illegal but often necessary to keep food on the table.) It seems that Ernest was riding horseback down the canyon when he came upon the Botts brothers thrashing about in the creek. After a short talk he discovered what they were trying to do. The creek was swollen with dirty water and the Botts boys had no luck catching a fish. Wet, cold, and unsuccessful in their fishing efforts, the Botts decided it was time to head home over the steep hill and up past the Klau Mine. Dusk was approaching and as the Botts were nearing the top of Santa Rosa Creek they heard sounds of horse hoofs coming up quickly. Concerned that they were going to get caught by a game warden for fishing, they quickly hid off to the side of the trail. After a few seconds of waiting, Ernest rode by with a huge steelhead tied to the horn of his saddle. Ernest had caught this fish for them and was trying to intercept them before they went down the Adelaida side of the mountain. The Botts didn't want to take Ernest's steelhead, but he insisted. Ernest said it was easier for him to catch a fish because he lived on the coast near the streams. This act of kindness made a considerable impression on the Botts family, and this story is still remembered. Joe Botts reminisced that the Botts family "never said a bad word about any Sotos."

Ernest was a fantastic horseman and liked to ride good horses. When Ernest was a young man, good horsemanship and well-trained horses were something a cowboy took pride in. However, Ernest was often teased about one particular horse that he rode. Friends said that this horse was trained to look for steelhead as it walked along the creek. The story goes that this special horse would walk alongside the creek, and when the horse spotted a steelhead, it was trained to stop and wait for the rider to get off and catch the fish. Maybe this was the horse Ernest was riding when he caught the fish for Jack Botts!

Ernest became somewhat of a philosopher in his later years. He would often think up witty ideas about different things, perhaps similar to Will Rogers. For example, Ernest thought the proper name for a station wagon should be an extension wagon. He also mentioned that a marriage license should cost thousands of dollars and a divorce only two dollars, not the other way around!

GRAND MARSHAL -- Ernest Soto, a native son of the North Coast, served as the honorary head of the 25th Pinedorado celebration this year and led one of the biggest and best parades up Main Street on Saturday morning. --Cambrian photo by Ralph Morgan.

Courtesy: The Cambrian
Ernest Soto (on Loco), 1973 Grand Marshall of Cambria Pinedorado

Ernest loved to drink coffee throughout the day (ten to twelve cups). He said it kept him "cool" on a hot day. He constantly asked visitors who came in the house if they wanted a cup of "C - O" (which was his term for coffee).

Ernest married Elsie Barlogio at the mission in San Luis Obispo, as chronicled in a June 7, 1973, *Cambrian* article about them:

In 1923, after a courtship that included many long horseback rides over the mountains from the upper reaches of Santa Rosa Creek down into Green Valley, Ernest Soto claimed Elsie Barlogio as his bride. With good natured banter that marks this fine couple she claimed that she was a "'child bride'" and he countered that she was quick to answer his proposal—which he had mailed in a letter.

Elsie was an amazing person. Although small in stature, she was huge in personality and determination. Nothing could stop Elsie or slow her down, not even the loss of a limb. Elsie lost her lower left leg from phlebitis after giving birth to her son, Vernon. The doctor instructed Elsie to stay in bed after childbirth for two weeks, without getting up and thus allowing her circulation to return. Upon returning home, Elsie soon began to suffer terrible leg pains and was finally forced back to the doctor. By this time, though, amputation was recommended as the only option. Elsie often spoke of her doctor as a "butcher."

In 1950, Elsie purchased her "home" ranch approximately six miles east of Cambria on Santa Rosa Creek Road. This beautiful 237-acre parcel was previously owned by John and Estelle Marquart. To pay for this land,

Elsie used inherited money from her recently deceased parents' estate, that of James Barlogio. Upon hearing that this desirable parcel was for sale, Elsie and Ernest drove down the canyon from the upper ranch to visit the Marquarts. While verbally making the deal to purchase this property the telephone rang and John Marquart answered it. Elsie could hear Mr. Marquart telling the other party (who turned out to be Edwin Soto, son of Barney Soto) that Elsie and Ernest Soto were there now and that they had just sealed the purchase of the ranch.

Courtesy: Robert Soto

Elsie and Ernest Soto; 1975

The history of this beautiful property is very interesting as remembered by Lillian Murphy, granddaughter of the original owner, James Monroe Buffum (1824-1889). Built in 1863, the original house was a two-room log cabin situated on the rocky hill slightly above the current house. In the late 1870s, Buffum then built the "salt box" home, which stood until the 1920s at the same place as my present-day home.

In 1889, James Buffum was kicked by a horse in the stomach. Severely injured, he suffered for three days while lying in bed in the upstairs bedroom. Lillian recalled:

> After James Monroe Buffum died in 1889, his family continued to live there until the property was sold to the Marquarts around 1910 or so.

GENERATION 6   133

Courtesy: Lillian Murphy

Buffum house; 1870s

Courtesy: Robert Soto

Home of Robert and Debbie Soto

John and Estelle Marquart constructed the current craftsman-style home in 1922. As recalled by Wilfred Lyons, life-long Cambria resident and historian, this beautiful house reportedly cost $5,000 to build, a price considered exorbitant for the times. The Marquarts lived on the ranch until the sale to Elsie Soto in 1950.

Elsie's nickname (it was very common for all the Sotos to have a nickname) was "Silk." Elsie acquired this name because she always handled things so smoothly. Elsie was always ready to cook meals at the last minute for family and friends. It was not at all uncommon for three or four people to show up unannounced at Elsie's doorstep right before lunch or dinner. Unconcerned by the sudden increase in guests, Elsie would quickly whip up a tasty meal for everyone.

Elsie also earned the nickname "Silk" by being coy and clever, but sometimes her cunning nature backfired. Each Thanksgiving the large Soto family gathered and shared good times, food, and drink. This was also when names for the upcoming Christmas gift exchange would be drawn. Each adult would buy one gift for the name drawn, and the surprise of not knowing who had your name was part of the fun. This particular Thanksgiving dinner was held at the home of Dona and Jim Soto (Andrew Soto's youngest son) in Morro Bay. Dona decided she would play a joke on everyone, so she secretly put only her name on all the tags for the drawing. Dona was considered a difficult person to buy for because she was accustomed to very nice things. As Dona passed the hat around so everyone could draw their Christmas name, there was a lot of moaning and complaining as each person secretly drew Dona's name. When Elsie finally drew, she announced she had drawn her own name and needed to draw again. Dona raised her eyebrows but let Elsie draw one more time. Elsie was very confused when she drew Dona's name for the second

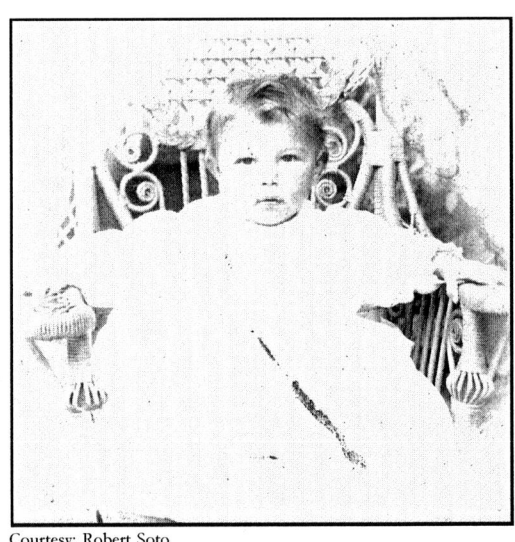
Courtesy: Robert Soto
Elsie (Barlogio) Soto; 1906

time, but she said nothing. Later, as people quietly confided with each other whose name they had drawn (Dona's), the joke was out and everyone had a good laugh. But the clever Elsie was caught in a "little white lie," as she had told Dona she drew her own name and needed to draw again for the second time.

Elsie was quite a prankster herself and loved a good joke. She played a prank on George Soto (1902-1968), the only son of Augustine "Gus" and Mary Warren Soto, when he worked for Ernest and Elsie while on the Summers Ranch. George was single and was courting a young woman living at the Lehman Ranch (today's Walter Ranch). At this time, communications were by telephone, and that was limited to an eight-party line. When anyone called on the party line, all the phones would ring but you were only to answer your specific ring. Somehow Elsie knew that the young girl of George's affection would not be home. At lunchtime, when George returned from working, he quickly went into Andrew's house to call this young woman. Elsie and Ernest, who lived about one mile above Andrew on the Summers

Courtesy: Karen (Soto) Snow
George "Chap" Soto horseback as a young man

place, heard the distinctive ring coming from George as he called the Lehman Ranch. Elsie was prepared for this joke when she answered the telephone, disguising her voice as George's girlfriend. When George began getting "lovey-dovey," Elsie burst out laughing. George realized it was Elsie instead of his girlfriend and slammed down the receiver. It was several days before George would speak to Elsie again.

George Soto (whose nickname was "Chap") was a hard-working, hard-drinking cowboy who was quite a character. The family always remembered George attending local dances and how he would wrap his hand with a clean handkerchief when touching the waist of his female dancing partners. This was to isolate the perspiration on his hand from the woman's clothing.

George had two sisters, Theresa and Calista Soto. George, Theresa, and Calista are all buried in the Cambria Catholic Cemetery.

In the Spanish-Mexican custom, the Soto family held many gatherings that were important for family bonding. In the early 1920s the families all gathered for Christmas at Barney and Margaret Soto's when they lived up Santa Rosa Creek on the old Lehman Ranch. Margaret said that she and Barney lived at the Lehman Ranch from 1917 to 1931, until Mr. Benton (Mrs. Benton was a Lehman) sold the property to Dee Fitzhugh for $80,000. The original Lehman house was constructed in 1875, after being homesteaded by the Lehman family.

Courtesy: Robert Soto
George Soto with "Miss Tuesday" at Elsie Soto Ranch; 1960

In 1869, John and Louisa Lehman settled on this rough mountainous ranch with their four children. They left Dayton, Ohio, along with two other related families, in search of a better climate and life for John, who was suffering from a serious illness. Their original destination was San Jose, but on hearing en route of the beautiful land available near Cambria, their plans changed. Over the course of several years, about 2,300 government acres were acquired by the Lehman family.

Stories abound regarding Lehman's early experiences in milking his wild cowherd. Mrs. Lehman was initially terrified of the mountains, and when the men were away, it became her job to milk these wild cows. She would dress in her husband's clothes and pull a hat over her face so the cows would think John was milking them.

The way of life was changing for the Californios. New laws regarding property began taking effect, laws they did not understand. Early incidents were common as many new settlers fenced off their property to keep "intruders" out. This was clearly revealed as a Lehman daughter wrote in Delmar Williams's book *Chronicles of Cambria's Pioneers* (1946):

> The Spaniards naturally resented the new settlers who began to gain title to the land and build fences. They would drive their stock onto my father's range and stand guard.

Another example of the negative feelings towards the native-born during this time was portrayed in *Chronicles of Cambria's Pioneers* when Rufus Olmsted's daughter recounted:

> Mrs. Olmsted tells of how her husband and sons were often gone from home for days, prospecting, leaving her and her young daughters alone. She relates that she never saw anybody but an occasional Spaniard or Indian, and that she suffered from fear, "God only knows how much!"

After Mrs. Lehman died in 1898 the ranch was renamed "Mountain Park" and was operated as a summer resort. Clients were met in Paso Robles and delivered to this magnificent mountain ranch to enjoy the unique vistas. The adult Lehman children kept the ranch until it was sold to Dee Fitzhugh.

When Barney and Margaret Soto lived in the Lehman house, Dolly Soto recalled going on Christmas Eve, as a little girl, to the large house on top of the mountain. After Soto's Market closed its doors for the evening, the Jack Soto family would drive up the Santa Rosa Creek canyon and, if it were wet and rainy, Uncle Barney would meet them at the main road with a horse-drawn open sled. It was a very long and hard trip up the steep, muddy incline to the big old house on the hill. Dolly recalled it being exciting when they got to ride in the open sled. The setting for this home was unique and etched in young Dolly's mind. The sled ride was a special treat for a young girl, and arriving at the huge home with its high ceilings was always memorable. Margaret recalls in a *Cambria-San Simeon Country News* article of December 17-23, 1980:

Courtesy: Terri Soto
Lehman house high up in the Mountains of Santa Rosa Creek; circa 1920s

There was always a big Christmas tree in the living room. We'd hear Santa Claus come up the road and the jingle bells. Everyone would get so excited when they heard the jingle bells. And Uncle Augustine [Gus] always gave us a silver dollar. We'd look forward to it. That's always what it was, a silver dollar.

Christmas dinner included the families of Cipriano, Barney, Gus, Jack, Andrew, and Ernest Soto. Dolly remembered that Cipriano and "the boys" had to leave after dinner so they could milk cows early the next morning. However, most of the families spent the night, sleeping over in the big house.

When morning came, Cipriano and his boys would return on horseback for a big Christmas breakfast. This was always a very special family gathering. Elsie Soto also recalled her first time attending Christmas at Barney's house on the Lehman Ranch. Her memories included seeing all the beautiful rolled-out raw dough she thought would be baked into hot dinner rolls. To her dismay, the Soto women began "patting" these rolls to make tortillas instead of dinner rolls. Elsie was disappointed when she realized that this family made tortillas instead of dinner rolls like her Swiss family. It should be noted, however, that Elsie also was a fantastic cook and perfected the Spanish-Mexican art of making flour tortillas. Quite a feat for a little Swiss lady!

Courtesy: Steven Soto

Neighboring ranchers at the "Lehman" Ranch; 1930s

Front row from Left: Cipriano Soto, George Warren, Laurence Mora, Sam Borradori, Abbott Fitzhugh, Elmer Fitzhugh, Tobias "Bias" Mora, Mrs. Caroline Fitzhugh, Barney Soto, Will Thomas Fitzhugh, Margaret Soto, Charlie Ebline, John Marquart

On Fence & Horseback: Cyril Thorndyke, Mr. McMillan, Will Warren, Johnny & Tilly Souza, Doris Ingles, ?, Archie Soto, Dee Fitzhugh

Beginning in the 1940s, Christmas celebrations were held at Elsie and Ernest's house at the Summers Ranch. In the 1950s and 1960s, all the Christmas parties were held at Elsie and Ernest's Marquart Ranch home. The house was full of family; a huge turkey dinner was traditional with all the trimmings. As a youth the house seemed huge to me. The fire in the brick fireplace was burning, and a Christmas tree dominated the living room. Presents were piled underneath the tree and even overflowed onto the exterior porch. Santa Claus always made an entrance (originally Elsie in costume, later Jim Soto), and many Soto children affirm that they saw his sled and heard the reindeer hooves on the roof. After Elsie and Ernest, Jim Soto began hosting family Christmas parties at the upper ranch until the late 1990s. This was the last time the entire family was together. Now, each individual family holds its own party.

Another traditional gathering in the Soto family was the first day of trout season. This fish party would fall on May first each year, and the celebration was always held at Andrew Soto's house on the upper ranch. Family and friends gathered for an evening meal, and then around dusk the poker games began. The Sotos loved to play cards, and on this evening the poker lasted until dawn. At sunrise everyone went fishing and returned for a big trout breakfast.

Besides taking care of everyone on the ranch, hosting many dinners and family parties, Elsie also worked in the Coast Union High School cafeteria for many years. In fact, her goal was to work until both her grandchildren were out of school. Her objective completed, she retired in 1968 after I graduated from Coast Union.

Courtesy: Robert Soto

Elsie Soto and son, Vernon, on raft at Dry Bones; 1935

The child of Ernest and Elsie (Barlogio) Soto is:

1. **Vernon Ernest Soto**   b. 1925
    m. 1945 Althea Lorraine Smithers   b. 1926

GENERATION 7 (VERNON)

Courtesy: Robert Soto
Vernon Soto on horseback at upper Summers Ranch; 1945

Vernon was born in 1925 while his parents lived on the Summers Ranch. Having been born into ranch life, he loved all the freedom it allowed. As a young boy and only child, Vernon was always around the cowboys and other adults. During this time it was common among many of the cowboys to use colorful language when talking with each other. It was only natural that some of this language would rub off on Vernon. Because of this, Vernon was often caught swearing by Elsie, his mother. Elsie warned him that she would wash his mouth out with soap if he kept swearing. Alas, Elsie soon had Vernon outside blowing bubbles with a bar of soap in his mouth, to which he said, "I'll eat that tunny-bitchen soap." A lesson on swearing may not have been learned, but the Soto family always remembers young Vernon's comment.

Vernon attended grammar school at Mammoth Rock, a one-room schoolhouse on upper Santa Rosa Creek Road. A teacher he vividly remembers was Muriel Soto (Archie Soto's wife). Muriel was known for her sternness and no-tolerance attitude.

When Vernon was a young child attending school, he often rode horseback down the canyon to the Mammoth Rock schoolhouse. One rainy winter day Elsie drove the car to pick up Vernon and his cousin Andrew, Jr. (known as "Snow") from school. She had many groceries to carry home from where the car had to be parked (due to the muddy conditions). The two boys, trying to be helpful, decided they would run home and get a horse for Elsie to ride. This idea would save a mile's walk through the mud. When they returned with the horse, Elsie was surprised that they hadn't saddled it for her, but she never mentioned this to the boys. Nevertheless, she climbed up on the horse bareback, carrying a couple of sacks of groceries. Both boys were walking alongside the horse when it lunged to cross a small gully during the violent rainstorm. This sudden move caught Elsie off guard, and she had difficulty balancing bareback because of having only one leg. She was left lying in the grimy roadway with groceries scattered all over in the mud. The boys wasted little time in pushing her back up on the horse, picking up the groceries, and heading up the mountainous canyon towards home. This story was always remembered by Vernon, who never forgot how badly he felt for his mother falling off the horse.

In 1940 at age fourteen, Vernon began working as a cowboy for the main Hearst Ranch in San Simeon. The cow boss at this time was Archie

Soto. Many Sotos also worked as cowboys for the Hearst Ranch, including the brothers Cipriano, Gus, Barney, and Joaquin (Jack).

Andrew "Snow" Soto (1925-2011) grew up living with Elsie and Ernest because his mother, Violet (Ingles) Soto, died in 1938, when Snow was thirteen. Carol Soto (b. 1929), was eight years old then, and young Jim Soto (b. 1933) was just four. It was decided that both Snow and Carol would live with Elsie and Ernest, while Jim would live with his grandparents, Cipriano and Carmel Soto. Because of this, Jim developed a unique bond with his grandparents since they took special care of him.

Jim recently recalled when his mother first became ill in late 1937; Andrew took him to the lower Hearst Ranch San Simeon Creek home of Cipriano Soto to stay with his grandparents. This occurred during the winter months, and San Simeon Creek was roaring from heavy runoff after several days of torrential rains. Young Jim remembers being literally handed over from father Andrew to his grandfather Cipriano. Both men were on horseback, for there was no bridge to cross San Simeon Creek at this time. On Cipriano's trip home with young Jim, they crossed the swollen raging creek, both seated on the one saddle; the horse went down submerged in the murky water and was forced to swim against the powerful river. The current carried the horse with Cipriano and Jim downstream until it finally regained its footing and fought its way up the soggy river bank to firm ground. This dramatic crossing was seared into young Jim's mind.

Jim then shared old memories that weeks later he attended Violet's (his mother's) funeral. Cipriano hooked up the heavy hay wagon to the large workhorses, with Cipriano at the reins; his wife, Carmel, daughter Evelyn, and young Jim climbed onto the hay wagon's high seat in preparation to cross San Simeon Creek. As the huge horses descended into the raging muddy waters, they again lost their footing in a gravel area that had been washed out. This deep hole in the creek basin was impossible to visualize because of the murky water. Jim remembered seeing the horses go down into the wash and nearly out of sight. Because the heavy work wagon was coupled to the team of horses, it soon began to float and drift downstream. Struggling for their life, the workhorses fought to regain their footing and finally pulled themselves up the steep creek bank with the large wagon in tow. Jim remembered that both Carmel and Evelyn tightly held on to him during this traumatic crossing, but he also recalls that Cipriano was in calm control during this tense situation.

Courtesy: Jim Soto
Cipriano with grandson Jim Soto, up the Coast on the Hearst Ranch; 1943

When Vernon was a young boy he often spent time with his grandparents Cipriano and Carmel. These were important times for Vernon and he developed a very close relationship with them. In 1941, when Cipriano lived up the coast near San Carpojo Creek on the Hearst Ranch, Vernon would occasionally stay with his grandparents for several weeks at a time. Money was scarce but food was plentiful. Occasionally, Carmel would ask the boys to go down to the ocean and get abalone or fish for dinner. They would take only what could be eaten that evening. But what Vernon enjoyed most was the frequent deer hunting. Because there was no refrigeration, meat was dried into jerky to preserve it. To provide food for the table, Carmel would ask the boys to kill a deer for meat each week. This occurred year round, and there was little consideration for the legal deer season, which officially began in August.

One summer day when young Vernon was staying up the coast at San Carpojo, Carmel asked him to shoot a deer. He saddled his horse and went back into the mountains. He soon came upon some deer and selected one in good condition to shoot. After field-dressing the deer, he loaded it on his horse to take back to the ranch house. However, as Vernon reached the top of the hill overlooking the house, he noticed a car parked at the house. Because this wasn't legal deer season, he decided to tie up his horse with the deer strapped onto the saddle and walk down to the house to see who the visitor was. After he reached the house he discovered that the guests were family, so he decided it was all right to bring the horse and deer home. When he went back up the hill to retrieve the horse, he realized it had broken loose and was now grazing alongside Highway 1, with the illegal deer strapped to the saddle! Although there were few cars at that time, anyone driving by could easily see the horse and what it was carrying. Vernon quickly ran down to the road, grabbed the horse, and brought it back to the house so the deer could be cleaned and cut up. This was a scare that he never forgot.

Courtesy: Carol (Soto) Lowry
Young Vernon and Carol (Soto) Lowry coon hunting at old Summers house; circa 1937

Vernon recalled the story about how Johnny Reis (whose family once lived at the Timbers) was shot near the corral on the Summers Ranch. Vernon was a young boy living at the upper ranch when other boys came to play. Two older boys, from the Lewis family, went ahead to shoot their .22 rifles. Elsie told the three younger boys, Vernon, Snow (Andrew, Jr.), and Johnny Reis, that the two older boys were shooting and that the young boys were not to cross the creek and walk up the hill towards the shooters. But being young boys they disregarded the instructions and immediately crossed the creek while heading up the hill. Vernon was in the middle of the three boys when he recalled hearing the shot and the "werrrr" of the bullet heading towards them. The .22 bullet hit a rock and ricocheted towards the young boys. Johnny Reis let out a scream, and when the boys looked around they saw blood on the side of his shirt. The older boys heard the scream and ran down the hill to investigate. They came upon young Johnny lying on the ground, writhing in pain. In frustration, Billy Lewis took his prized .22 rifle and broke it in half by smashing it over nearby rocks. Johnny Reis was taken to the local doctor, but because of where the bullet was lodged, it was not removed. Johnny carried this bullet to his grave some seventy years later.

As previously mentioned, during the Depression years the Ernest Soto family was forced to move into San Luis Obispo so that Ernest could earn necessary wages. Elsie and Ernest, with their son Vernon, rented a small house at 486 Marsh Street in San Luis. After living there for about two years, and with the Depression finally improving, Ernest was able to move his family back to the home ranch on upper Santa Rosa Creek.

Vernon was an excellent cowboy and roper. As a youth his passion was roping. He tells the story of how he and Snow sneaked over to the neighbor's ranch to rope their calves (Mora Ranch, the present-day Jackson Ranch) when he knew the Moras would be gone. The two youths were having fun roping the little calves and stretching them out. The calves began to "beller and bawl" since they didn't enjoy this as much as the ropers did. All of a sudden the fun ended when the neighbor's hired man (who the young boys had forgotten about) came out of the bunkhouse and hollered at them, "What in the hell are you kids doing?" In haste, Vernon and Snow made a fast trip home.

Vernon entered many rodeos as a young man. Cambria was well-known for its rodeos, dating back to 1900. The first rodeos where held at

Early-day Cambria Rodeo at Phelan Grove; circa 1930

Phelan's Canyon in the Cambria pines from 1900 to about 1926. In the early days, wild stock from the Hearst San Simeon Piedra Blanca Ranch would be driven down the coast into Cambria for use at the local rodeo. The next place for the Cambria rodeo was at Phelan's Grove, up in the pines near the community cemetery. This was a huge event that often lasted over a three-day weekend. It included barbecues, a parade, dances on Friday and Saturday night, and, of course, the rodeo itself. The following 1935 Cambria Rodeo pamphlet mentions the Phelan's Grove Rodeo as being the eighth annual event, thus making 1927 the first year it was held there (although many events were held earlier in this pine-covered meadow). The officials of the day were very prominent people in early Cambria and San Luis Obispo County. Senators, assemblymen, judges, and county supervisors are listed. The "Marshall of the Day" was Don Pancho Estrada from San Simeon. Also one of the "pick up" men was Barney Soto, who was working at the Piedra Blanca Hearst Ranch. One of the timers was John Marquart, the rancher from whom Elsie later purchased her home ranch in 1950. Admission to the rodeo was $1.10 for a full day's entertainment.

The inside of this pamphlet described the rodeo events in detail and promised a good time for all. Cipriano Soto often participated in "Best Reined Horse" and "Best Hackamore Horse" events. These events showcased a cowboy's true horsemanship skills, allowing Cipriano to excel.

Vernon has many memories of roping with his grandfather. Vernon entered many of the roping events, including steer stopping and team roping, which were events for youthful men. A "Big Cowboy Dance" was scheduled for both Saturday and Sunday nights in the town of Cambria.

Later, the rodeos would be moved behind today's Brambles Restaurant in what locals still call the Rodeo Grounds. This area was situated on a large flat adjacent to Santa Rosa Creek and today's Highway 1, across from the present-day Catholic Church. Vernon proudly recalls one particular roping event held at Edna (near San Luis Obispo), where he won first place and Gene Rambo, the five-time world champion, came in second.

Locally, horse trailers weren't yet readily available, making it difficult to travel and participate in events. A neighboring cattle rancher, William

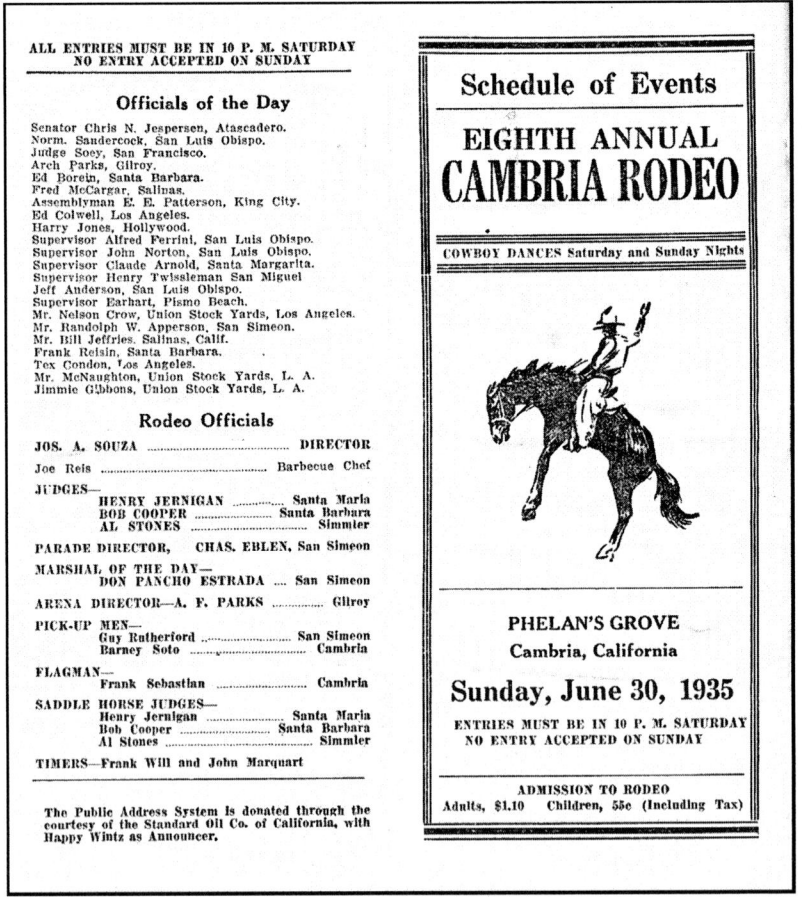

Courtesy: Robert Soto
Pamphlet from Cambria Rodeo held at Phelan's Grove; 1935

GENERATION 7   149

Early-day Cambria Rodeo Grounds; circa 1940s

Courtesy: Jim Soto
Cambria Rodeo float, San Luis Obispo La Fiesta de las Flores Parade; 1948

Hartzell, recalled seeing long strings of horses tied from head to tail meandering through the coastal mountains, heading down to Cambria. This was the only way to transport the rodeo horses prior to good roads and horse trailers. Cowboys would be in front and in back of this string, leading the horses across the rough terrain and down into the low-lying town of Cambria. What a sight this must have been! The cowboys simply went through each adjacent ranch, using the barbed-wire fence gates for access until they arrived at their destination. The horses must have been well-trained and quite accustomed to this type of travel.

Bill Hartzell also mentioned that each small town held a rodeo and that cowboys could participate locally nearly every weekend if they wanted to. Entry fees were minimal, allowing many ranchers to join in the fun and test their skills.

In 1945, when Vernon and Althea Smithers were married, they lived in a large two-story house in Green Valley (presently the Taylor house). They farmed and milked cows on this property, along with Vernon's first cousin Snow and his wife, Bonnie (Whitlock) Soto. Approximately 110 cows were milked in the winter months by the two young, industrious men. When Snow and Bonnie married, they also moved into this house with Vernon and Althea. The large house provided separate quarters for Snow and Bonnie, who lived upstairs. In 1952, Vernon, Althea, and by now their two children moved up to the Lehman Ranch, about eight miles up Santa Rosa Creek. There were two homes on this mountain parcel, and

Courtesy: Robert Soto

Vernon and Althea Soto, Summers Ranch; 1946

Vernon and his family lived in the smaller one-story home. At this time, Vernon was working for his father, Ernest, and his uncle Andrew on the home ranch. However, Ernest and Andrew weren't able to pay adequate wages for Vernon's young family to survive.

Vernon began working for Constantine Fiscalini from 1954 until about 1965. Vernon and his family then moved to lower Santa Rosa Creek, across from Olympio Fiscalini. A crossing allowed them to drive across the creek to the large two-story house until the heavy winter rains washed out the roadway. Then the only way across the raging creek was a "swinging" cable footbridge. This could be challenging at night, during rainstorms, while carrying groceries, and with two small children.

Courtesy: Kathleen (Fiscalini) Gerhardt
Neighbor Olympio Fiscalini with children Kathleen and Alfred, Santa Rosa Creek, beneath the swinging bridge; 1940

About 1950, Ernest and Andrew Soto purchased the Rotanzi Ranch, north of Villa Creek on the ocean side of Highway 1. This ranch currently shares the southern border with the State of California's new Harmony Headlands park property. At roughly five hundred acres, this coastal parcel provided considerable ocean frontage, but as a cattle ranch it was only marginal. The Rotanzi Ranch was soon turned over and operated by "the boys," Vernon and Snow. Snow and his family moved into the old house on the northeast side of the hill, facing Highway 1. It was while living at the Rotanzi Ranch that Snow declared that this was where "fog was made."

This coastal ranch often had heavy wet fog, quite different from the weather up Santa Rosa Creek. The Rotanzi Ranch was sold in 1964, inasmuch as ocean frontage was becoming relatively valuable.

Courtesy: Steven Soto
Snow, Steven, Bonnie, Andrew and Cipriano, Rotanzi Ranch; 1952

When Vernon raised cattle on the Rotanzi Ranch, an older Chinese man lived there alone in a small, dilapidated wooden shack, alongside the majestic Pacific Ocean. The Soto family can recall seeing him working on the rocks, harvesting seaweed to ship to San Francisco. Although he didn't speak English well, How Wong was able to communicate effectively through sign language and by using an occasional English word. When the Rotanzi Ranch was purchased, How Wong came with the land. He paid his rent for living on the property in cases of Chinese candy, leachee nuts, and dried seafood. These foods were authentic; all the boxes had Chinese labeling only, no English writing. These items were very unusual, and some of them emitted strange odors. As a result, the family was often too scared to eat the dried seafood, but everyone loved the candy!

Courtesy: Geneva Hamilton
How Wong's house next to Pacific Ocean

One day, in the early 1960s, How Wong got a message to Vernon that a steer had fallen off a cliff from a very steep bluff and onto the beach. This steer was now without fresh water or grass, and it would not survive long in those conditions. Vernon quickly gathered up some friends, including neighbors Alfred and Olie Fiscalini, Jr., to help catch and bring this steer up the bank and back to safety. The steer became excited when it saw the rescue crew descend down the narrow path, making their way towards him. In a bolt, the steer dove into the pounding surf and began swimming out to sea. Vernon quickly recognized the danger and ran out into the water after the steer, swinging his trusty rope. In a flash, all of Vernon's ranch training proved successful as he quickly lassoed the steer and pulled it back to shore.

Once on the beach, the men regrouped and repositioned ropes around the steer so as not to harm it; then they began the arduous task of pulling and pushing the steer back up the narrow beach trail to safety. After an exhausting rescue effort, the ropes were released and the steer was once again free to roam the ocean ranch.

Family members vividly recall this strange rescue and how hard the neighbors worked to liberate the steer. Vernon expertly roped the steer, given only one chance when it began swimming out to sea. If he failed, the steer would surely have drowned in the treacherous surf.

In the early 1960s, after Ernest retired, Vernon became partners with Andrew Soto in the upper ranch. Soon Andrew sold his interest in the cattle operation to his son-in-law, Bob Lowry, Carol (Soto) Lowry's husband. Vernon and Bob operated the ranch together until 1975, when Bob sold his half interest to yours truly, Bobby Soto.

Vernon and Bob Lowry ran cows together for about twelve years on the upper ranch and also at the Summers place. One fall day, the two men decided to go to the cattle sale at Templeton to purchase some calves. They took the 1950 green GMC one-ton cattle truck. This rickety old truck had been used for many years on the ranch and showed its heavy usage. The wooden racks on the eight-foot flatbed were loose and well-worn. After buying several young calves at the sale, it was time to head home over the extremely steep and winding Santa Rosa Creek Road. The men remembered first to stop at Pesenti Winery to buy a case of red zinfandel wine, as per Ernest's instructions. There were few wineries in the area at this time—Pesenti, Rotta, and York Mountain. Ernest was friends with the Pesenti family, preferred their red wine to the competitors, and their winery was right on the way home.

The wooden case, filled with four one-gallon glass jugs, was loaded on the floorboards of the old GMC when Vernon and Bob left for home. When climbing over the last steep grade before dropping into Santa Rosa Valley, the engine began to bog down, and Bob was forced to downshift into low gear. However, he was prevented from downshifting because the wooden case filled with wine was in the way. The cattle truck lost speed and began rolling backwards down the steep hill; quickly, Bob pushed the case of wine out of the way and successfully found low gear. But when the clutch was engaged, the truck lurched forward, sending all the cattle towards the back of the cattle racks. The weak sideboards couldn't hold this excessive pressure, and the cattle tumbled out of the truck. They rolled down the steep hill until finally getting to their feet. The wild and frightened cattle scattered, through the fences and down the roadway. Cattle went everywhere! It took several months to locate the newly purchased cattle, but eventually all were found and taken home. All this excitement and extra work for a case of wine!

In the late 1960s, Vernon purchased a 450-acre ranch (El Monte) from the Edmondo Barlogio estate. This land included the Mammoth Rock schoolhouse, which Vernon had attended. Edmondo, brother of Elsie, purchased this ranch in 1955 from Hulda Washburn (who had previously purchased it from the Thorndyke family). To buy the ranch, Vernon borrowed money from a Cayucos rancher and friend, Elmo Farrari. When this ranch came up for sale, Vernon believed it was overpriced, but Elmo advised him to buy it. What a wise decision!

Vernon loved ranch life and was honored to be elected to the San Luis Obispo County Cattlemen's Board for several years. In 1999, he was selected by his peers as County Cattleman of the Year. He greatly treasures this special recognition.

Vernon loved to gamble and was very proficient at cards and dice (craps). He enjoyed trips to Las Vegas or Laughlin, Nevada, to practice his skills. Locally, he had a reputation as a gambler and was considered "lucky." However, he seriously studied all the odds and only bet when the odds were in his favor, so this was not considered luck to him. He went on many of the San Luis Obispo Caballero trail rides over the three-day Memorial Day weekends. This was a men-only horseback ride full of drinking, gambling, socializing, and great fun for Vernon. He typically won money more often than he lost it during these outings.

In 1961, Vernon and his wife, Althea, purchased three acres from his mother, Elsie Soto, at the former Marquart place and built their dream home. This peaceful setting allowed Vernon to plant avocado, citrus, and other fruit trees. Althea was one of seven children born to Lester Smithers (1899-1938) and Gladys (Kester) Smithers (1902-1987).

The Smithers family was raised on the present-day Leimert housing tract in Cambria. Lester died an early death from a ruptured appendix. The loss of their father created many hardships for the Smithers family, and in the 1960s they were forced to sell their Cambria ranch property to developer Walter Leimert. This beautiful property became the premier residential area for Cambrians.

The original Smithers Ranch was purchased in two parcels. The "home" parcel was purchased by Amos Smithers (Lester's father). This parcel had a house and barn and was considered home, where he milked his famous Jersey cows. Amos also purchased property across Santa Rosa Creek in downtown Cambria, land that was later turned over to his son "Friday."

During World War II, Lester's son, "Dutch," was stationed in England. Dutch sent home all the money he made to his mother, Gladys. She took this money and, at Dutch's request, purchased the adjoining Berginini place. Now the home ranch consisted of approximately five hundred acres.

The father of Lester Smithers, Amos Smithers (1851-1932), was the president of the Bank of Cambria. Beginning in 1901, he owned and lived in the present-day Oallieberry Inn on Cambria's Main Street. Amos, who owned substantial property, was married to Ida Marcia Terrill (1856-1914), whose parents were Samuel Newell Terrill (1822-1857) and Roxana Matilda Leffingwell (1836-1913).

The maternal grandparents of my mother, Althea, were Ed Kester (1877-1958) and Lucy (McKeon) Kester (1876-1961), who lived in Cambria across the street from the Brambles Restaurant. They also lived next door to Jack and Agnes Soto. Ed Kester worked as a cowboy on the San Simeon Hearst Ranch. He would often drive to work with Barney Soto early Monday morning, stay at the ranch during the week, and return home on Saturday night. (Barney and Margaret Soto lived across today's Burton Drive in a large two-story house, next to the Squibb house.) The workweek for a Hearst Ranch cowboy was Monday through Saturday.

Courtesy: Althea (Smithers) Soto

Ed and Lucy Kester, 50th Wedding Anniversary, Smithers Ranch; early 1950s

The Kester family came from the Adelaida area, and according to J. Fraser MacGillivray's *The Story of Adelaida* (1992) was related to several pioneering families including the McKeons, Wrights, and Powells. Althea recalls her grandmother Lucy taking in laundry from neighbors to earn extra money. She had a washing machine in a detached shed in her backyard. I can recall visits with Grandma Lucy Kester every Sunday for dinner when she was quite elderly. Typically, the menu always included fried chicken. Her backyard was very large, with many chickens, vegetables, and berry vines.

The Lester Smithers family suffered many hardships with illnesses and the early deaths of several children. Dutch died at age fifty-seven after a prolonged illness caused by cancer. Bill died at fifty-eight from colon cancer, and Eldon was only five years old when he died of rheumatic fever. The youngest daughter, Marlene, died in a tragic car accident at the age of nineteen.

Althea was the third-born and oldest girl of the Smithers children. Although she recalls her childhood as "bleak," the Christmas holiday was very special. During the holiday season, they would go out into the forest and pick a native pine tree to decorate. One year, Althea recalled hearing that her two older brothers were getting brand new bicycles for Christmas. She also wanted one and asked her father for this special gift. Her father said he could only afford two bikes, not three. This hurt Althea's feelings, and yet when Christmas came, a third shiny new blue and silver bicycle was under the tree for her. This was a very special Christmas for her because the following year, 1938, her father died at the age of thirty-nine. Her younger sister Shirley also wanted a bicycle, but she only got a scooter.

One happy childhood memory for Althea was when the children would all take pails out into the pines and pick wild strawberries. In those days the strawberries were plentiful and considered a special treat. The children

Courtesy: Althea (Smithers) Soto
Ervin, Lester "Dutch," Althea "Polly," and Shirley Smithers, Smithers Ranch; 1934

would pick all they could eat and would also have some left over for homemade ice cream after supper.

In June 1944, during the peak of World War II, Althea and four young women in her graduating class from Coast Union High School ventured to Burbank to work at the huge Lockheed aerospace plant. They all got jobs, but some of the girls became homesick and quickly returned to Cambria while others left for college. Althea and only one other local girl remained for the entire season. Althea worked on riveting the wings of B-17 airplanes.

Courtesy: Roberta (Goodall) Galbriath
Cambria "Rosie the Riveters"; from left, Ethel Camozzi, BJ Lownes, Roberta Goodall, Betty Soto, and Althea Smithers

Althea's older brother Dutch was a mechanic on airplanes in England and often teased her about losing so many of the B-17s to German fire. Dutch said the planes were big and slow, and the enemy easily shot them out of the sky. However, Althea always felt Dutch was secretly proud that his sister worked on these planes as a true "Rosie the Riveter."

Althea's uncle Ernest "Friday" never married. Friday reportedly was tagged with this nickname because he worked only on Fridays at W.M. Lyon's Red & White grocery store. He later owned and lived in a small house near Santa Rosa Creek, adjacent to today's "Tin City" area. The only access to this area was by a narrow wooden swinging footbridge that crossed Santa Rosa Creek. This bridge was near the Oallieberry Inn.

Courtesy: Althea (Smithers) Soto
Footbridge crossing Santa Rosa Creek, Cambria

Friday was often spotted sitting in his car in downtown Cambria with a friend, Cambria Constable "Boots" Blake. It seems they both enjoyed an occasional drink, and since Boots Blake didn't have a vehicle and couldn't drive, Friday would assist him with apprehending Cambria criminals. In the early 1950s, when Friday died, Lloyd Junge (a rancher and cowboy on the Hearst Ranch) came to young Dutch Smithers and explained that he'd been in the process of purchasing Friday's property. In those days land wasn't very valuable, so Dutch drew up the papers, probably received some money, and signed over this now-desirable land to Mr. Junge.

Shirley Smithers recalled her brother Dutch building a "buggy" as a young boy. This contraption had no braking system and used ropes for steering. The wheels were large, enabling it to go quite fast down the steep

Cambria hills. On the buggy's maiden voyage on their ranch, all the children helped push it up the steep hill near the old water tank. With Dutch behind the steering system, each child—Shirley, Althea, Eldon, Marlene, and Bill—got in. Down the steep hill they went, bouncing over every cow trail they crossed. Soon Dutch realized that the steering didn't work properly, and since there was no braking system, they were in serious trouble. As they headed down the embankment, they continued to gain speed, and soon a barbed-wire fence was directly in their path. They went right through the fence until they finally crashed to a stop. All the children tumbled out, and some were seriously hurt. Shirley continues to carry a scar from the sharp barbed wire to this day.

Courtesy: Althea (Smithers) Soto

Althea Smithers, Coast Union High School; 1944

Althea enjoyed cooking and was widely known in the Soto family as an excellent cook. She was also interested in gardening and caring for her yard. She was very content to stay at home and work around the house or outside in her yard. Being raised in the country, she always seemed to find more work to do than time to do it in.

After Vernon and Althea's wedding ceremony in 1945, a large shiveree was held for them before they moved into their Green Valley home. This party was put on by Elsie and held in the vacant Olmstead School building near their home. All the family, friends, and neighbors attended this great event.

The marriage of Vernon and Althea, who had been high school sweethearts, produced two children—Shirlene Ann Soto, born in 1947, and a son, Robert Vernon Soto, born in 1950. Shirlene married Walter Elliott in 1985, and I married Debra Mae Gerhardt in 1979. Debbie and I have two children—Monte Robert Soto, born in 1982, and a daughter, Melissa Mae Soto, born in 1984.

Shirlene excelled in school. In her senior year at Coast Union High School, she was student body president and valedictorian. She attended Santa Clara University and transferred to San Francisco State University, graduating from San Francisco State in 1969. At the University of New Mexico, she received her Doctorate in Latin American History. Shirlene was a professor at several universities, among them California State Polytechnic University, California State University of Northridge, and the University of California at Los Angeles. Two books were authored by her on the subject of Mexican-American women's history and struggles in early California. She was highly respected in her field and considered an authority on Mexican-American history. She was extremely helpful with this book about the Soto family because of her love of history and her special knowledge of the subject.

Shirlene and Walter Elliott enjoyed traveling the world. They traveled extensively in South America and Mexico because both were fluent in Spanish. They also enjoyed traveling to China, Europe, Russia, and Egypt. Shirlene and Walt lived most of their married lives in the Los Angeles area, but eventually they retired to their dream home in Los Osos to be closer to the Soto family.

On October 23, 2009, tragedy struck the Sotos when Shirlene and her husband were killed in a head-on collision while en route to Los Angeles. The memorial services were well-attended, with speakers remembering Shirlene's sweet and caring personality. This very accomplished woman was taken from our family at a much too early age.

Courtesy: Robert Soto
Vernon and Shirlene riding in the 1953 Pinedorado Parade

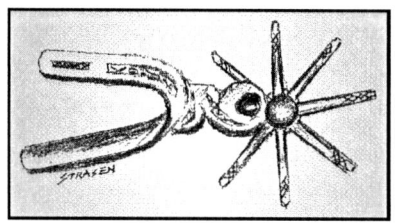

GENERATION 8 (ROBERT)

I was born on June 27, 1950, in the old French Hospital at 1160 Marsh Street in San Luis Obispo. June must have been a busy month for babies, because the delivery room was not available for Althea. She was temporarily placed on a wheeled bed in the hallway of the hospital until a room became available. Nonetheless, I decided not to wait and the delivery quickly began. Vernon desperately tried to find any available nurse to assist, but no one was able to help. When the situation grew tense, he went

Courtesy: Robert Soto

Robert Soto roping calves, El Monte Ranch; 1991

upstairs, found a nurse (not working in delivery), grabbed her by the arm and said, "You are coming with me." She wasn't allowed to work on the first floor but had little choice since she was being dragged downstairs by Vernon. Once the nurse discovered how far advanced Althea was, she quickly wheeled her into the only available room, a nearby broom closet. The nurse then went for a doctor, delivery being imminent. In the meantime, a janitor walked into the utility room, only to find a woman giving birth in his broom closet. What a shock that must have been! The doctor finally arrived, and I was quickly born. When the billing came for the hospital charges, delivery room fees had been included. Needless to say, Vernon was able to convince the hospital to delete those charges.

Courtesy: Althea (Smithers) Soto

Three-year-old Robert "Bobby" roping his first calf at the Lehman Ranch; 1953

I was very active in sports while attending Coast Union High School. Football, basketball, and baseball kept me busy; in addition, I was student body president in 1968. Attending a small school afforded many advantages and unique opportunities. The small, antiquated gymnasium was condemned because of California earthquake concerns, thus allowing my senior class of forty-four students to graduate at the prestigious Hearst Castle. This was a very special circumstance that hasn't occurred again.

As a young boy I always helped my father with cattle, building fence, and everything else necessary to operate the ranch. One story vividly recalled was that of bringing a herd of bulls down Santa Rosa Creek Road each December from Maccachi Camp to the "Dip." The area where you enter the upper Soto Ranch is called the Dip because there once was an old concrete vat that the cattle would be driven through to kill ticks and lice. An old stagecoach stop, adjacent to the huge eucalyptus trees, was also at the Dip. This area was the final stop heading up and over Santa Rosa Creek before climbing the mountains towards Templeton.

There were eight bulls, usually horned Herefords that would graze all summer and fall at Maccachi Camp. When it was time to gather the bulls, four or five cowboys would ride horseback and bring them down the paved road. This was an exciting event because the bulls could sense what was waiting for them (the cows) and would often fight in anticipation. To prevent the fighting we would keep the bulls in groups of one or two and separate each group with a cowboy on horseback. Sometimes, however, the bulls would slip down into the creek or trees to escape so they could fight with the next bull. It seems as though no matter how much we tried to separate the bulls, they eventually would fight. During this trip down the steep canyon road, the loud bellowing of the bulls could be heard for miles. These bulls fought ferociously, inasmuch as the winners would establish their dominant position with the cows.

One day someone stopped at the house and reported that there were ten to fifteen steers on the public road. Debbie and I drove up the road until we met the group of steers that had escaped from Maccachi Camp. We tried to drive them back up the road but they crossed the creek and instead went up an extremely steep hill near a concrete bridge across from Jackson's gate. I tried to get ahead of them but was unable to because of the brush and steepness of the hill. The bunch of steers, in single file, headed up through the thick brush until they could climb no more. The first steer finally came to a sheer cliff that dropped some twenty-five feet straight down to the paved roadway beneath. When the first steer stopped, the rest of the herd kept going, forcing the first steer forward and off the ledge; he tumbled down to the hard roadway beneath. The second steer was also forced ahead but got caught in the branches of a small tree that was hanging over the roadway. This steer was completely stuck in the branches of this tree; all four of his feet were suspended in mid-air and he couldn't get his footing. Debbie rushed home hoping to find our son, Monte, and to bring back several ropes. When Monte and Debbie arrived, he and I crawled up to the steer and gently placed a rope over his head and one front leg. After several minutes of trying to pull the steer over backwards, we were finally able to pull him out of the tree and back to safety. Unfortunately, photos were not taken. Who would have believed that a steer could get stuck in the upper branches of a tree suspended over a twenty-five-foot drop?

I also remember hauling steers to the upper ranch using an old one-and-a-half ton cattle truck that Vernon purchased from Archie Soto's estate. This little Dodge truck only had a twelve-foot bed but was very useful around our mountainous ranch. One morning Vernon was driving up to the upper ranch with a load of cattle and with me in the passenger seat. As we slowly attempted to round a turn on a red-rock ranch road, Vernon continued to go straight. I shouted, "Look out!" and quickly glanced over to see Vernon holding the entire steering wheel, which was no longer connected to the steering column. The nut holding the steering wheel had worked loose, making it impossible to steer the cattle truck. Luckily, we were driving very slowly and easily made the stop. I re-attached the steering wheel, threaded the nut back on the column shaft, and off we went to finish the haul.

Debbie, Monte, Melissa, and I first lived on the old Thorndyke Ranch, now identified as "El Monte" (purchased from the Edmondo Barlogio estate by Vernon and Althea), about nine miles east of Cambria on Santa Rosa Creek Road. This little house had only a small bathroom that had been added on to the back porch. A wood stove was the only source of heat. The house was adjacent to a small tributary of Santa Rosa Creek, whose waters provided a lot of fun for the children. The roof was made of old corrugated galvanized metal, and there was a walnut tree hanging over it. Walnuts would often drop from the tree; hit the roof and roll down, making a very loud noise. In 1987, when Elsie Soto entered a rest-home facility, my family and I moved into Elsie's old Marquart house.

Courtesy: Robert Soto
Debbie, Melissa, Robert and Monte, El Monte Ranch; 1985

Upon graduation from Coast Union High School in 1968, I went to San Francisco State University. The decision to attend this school was partly influenced by my sister, Shirlene, since she was a senior at San Francisco State. Because of the ongoing Vietnam War, campus life was very turbulent and highly political in San Francisco. There were many protests on this liberal campus, placing it in the national spotlight. Huey Newton and the Black Panthers often visited the campus to give speeches. There were many physical clashes with students and police-tactical squads, finally resulting in the campus closing. Attending San Francisco State University was an eye-opener for me, and I soon realized how much I loved the ranch and rural life.

After attending San Francisco State for several months, I decided to move back to Cambria and continue my schooling at Cuesta College. During Cuesta's summer break in 1970, three high school friends and I took a summer-long trip to Western Europe. Close friends and classmates Neil Langley, Doug Wagnon, and Mike Hake left with me in June 1970, flying standby to New York and then to London aboard Icelandic Airlines. Upon landing in London, we quickly located the dealership where four new Triumph Bonneville 650cc motorcycles were purchased for $888 each. We traveled all over Europe, staying where we wanted and for as long as we wanted. Being students, money was in short supply, so we often camped alongside the roadway and ate locally made cheeses and bread. At summer's end, the bikes were shipped back to New York in crates, reassembled, and then driven across country to Cambria and sold for $1,000 apiece.

After graduating from Cuesta College in 1970, I transferred to and graduated from California State Polytechnic University in San Luis Obispo in 1972, with a degree in history and social science. While in college at Cal Poly, I was drafted into the Army during my senior year. Because I was a full-time student, I was able to receive a student deferment until graduation in 1972. These were very violent times in the world, since the Vietnam War was peaking. After graduation, I joined the California Army National Guard, and in February 1973 I was sent to Fort Dix, New Jersey, for basic training. I recall leaving Paso Robles airport in seventy-degree weather and landing in New York during a snowstorm. Upon graduation from basic training, I went to advanced training at Aberdeen Proving Grounds in Maryland. When this was completed, I moved back to California and somewhat of a normal life again. As a National Guard reservist, my military service continued for six years at Camp Roberts, north of Paso Robles.

In 1979, I married Debra Gerhardt in the Bethany United Church of Christ in Tioga, Illinois. Wayne Gerhardt, Debbie's father, was born and raised in Illinois to a farming family. Wayne was stationed at the Cambria Air Force Station when he met his future wife, Kathleen Fiscalini, from Cambria. In 1955, they married at the old Cayucos Catholic Church and returned to Illinois to farm until 1984, when they moved back to the Fiscalini family ranch and built their home on Santa Rosa Creek Road. Wayne and Kathy had two children, Debbie and Gary.

Debbie was raised on the Illinois farm, where the family milked cows and raised corn and soybeans. A few years after graduating from high school, she came west to work at Hearst Castle and lived with her grandmother Alice Fiscalini and uncles Olie and Eddie Fiscalini. Debbie and I were from two pioneering families and always knew each other, but it was while working at Hearst Castle that we fell in love. After courting for about a year, we were married in Illinois where Debbie's family and friends lived.

After marriage, Debbie worked several years as a bookkeeper at Coast Union High School. This was a job she enjoyed thoroughly, for she wasn't much older than the students. In 1982, she was forced to quit this position when she was nine months' pregnant. She felt fortunate to have been a full-time mother and did not work again until both children were older.

Debbie's next career was that of a travel agent for San Simeon Travel. She took pleasure in this occupation since it allowed her to escort groups to enticing places around the world. In 2007, she began operating her own travel agency and is currently associated with a large agency through the Internet.

My working career began in high school with my first job in 1965 at the Cambria Fountain, when I was fifteen years old. I started as a dishwasher ($1.35 an hour) and progressed over the summer to short-order cook ($1.50 an hour). Beginning in 1967, during high school and then college, I worked during the summer months at Hearst Castle. After working as a Park Aid for three six-month terms, the opportunity arose to work for the Office of Architecture and Construction as a laborer. This was union pay, $4.35 an hour, which in 1970 was considered an excellent wage. In 1975, the State was undergoing a re-organization that allowed me to begin my career in the position of Skilled Laborer. From this position I was promoted in 1977 to Restoration Specialist. I worked at several interesting places, which included San Juan Bautista State Park, Columbia State Park, and the historic blacksmith shop at Mission La Purisima.

In 1993, I was promoted to Restoration Supervisor and in 2000 promoted again to Restoration Supervisor II. (I was the only Restoration Supervisor II in the State of California at this time.) I had two separate lives—one as a cattle rancher and the other as a State employee working in restoration. Both careers were fun and rewarding, and I was able to work on many amazing projects at Hearst Castle. These included restoring the exterior tower lights for the night tours, revamping the greenhouses, making molds, applying gold leaf to the ornamental plaster work, replicating the Celestial tower windows, and restoring "C" House after the February 12, 1976, bombing incident (associated with the Symbionese Liberation Army and the kidnapping of Patty Hearst). These projects gave me a unique appreciation for history and art work. During the busiest times when State funds were plentiful, I had forty staff members working for me. Because of this background, I acquired extensive knowledge of the trades and learned how to complete the most unique and difficult construction and restoration projects.

At 10:22 a.m. on the morning of December 22, 2003, a few days before I retired from Hearst Castle, the San Simeon earthquake struck. I can vividly recall this dramatic event. I was outside when it hit, and I ran up to the outdoor Neptune Pool. Because of this severe 6.3 shaker, the pool had a series of waves crossing it and water splashing out. Also, because of the violent movement, the bells were ringing in the Celestial towers and there was total chaos on the tours. Everyone was trying to call out using their cell phones, which quickly jammed the cell system. The Castle has two monopine cell towers, but their capacity was limited to fifty calls at a time. The Castle was closed for a few days after the quake to evaluate the damage, which turned out to be minimal.

I worked for the California State Parks Department at Hearst Castle for thirty-one years, since 1967. Five Soto generations worked on the Hearst Ranch or at Hearst Castle (Cipriano, Ernest, Vernon, myself, and Monte). I retired at the end of 2003 and began working full-time on the family ranch.

After retirement from the Castle, all of my efforts were concentrated on the family cattle ranch. This kept me very busy thanks to the huge backlog of unfinished projects that had accumulated over the years. Monte has been very helpful with these projects and also enjoys working outside with me. Projects included: building new steel pipe corrals, re-building the wood bridge, building fences, installing culverts, stabilizing barns, building roads, and improving water systems.

On November 14, 2009, Monte and I moved a herd of heifer calves to the Summers field at the upper ranch. Because of the recent death of my sister, Shirlene, I didn't ride my new horse, Tobasco, for a three-week period. This extended stretch of time allowed the spirited young horse too much energy, so when I was heading off a group of cattle, young Tobasco simply ducked his head and began bucking down an extremely steep hill. Unable to pull Tobasco's head up, I was thrown to the hard ground and the result was a split pelvis. This same type of accident befell my grandfather Ernest Soto in 1935. After a difficult eight-week recovery period, I continue to heal.

GENERATION 8   171

APPENDIX X

Soto Family Tree

27 Jun 2007

General H. SOTO [4]
Born 11 Sep 1830   #300
Marr abt 1869
Died 03 May 1906

Dolores GRAHALVA
Born Apr 1856   #395
Died 03 Jan 1923

Cipriano SOTO [5]
Born 16 Sep 1870   #330
Jolon, Monterey Co., California
Marr 11 May 1895
Mission de San Luis, #8095
Died 28 Jul 1956
San Luis Obispo, California

Anastacio ASEBEZ
Born 24 Apr 1826   #200
Marr abt 1869/70
Died 01 Mar 1906

Placida V. GARCIA
Born Feb 1853   #60
Died Nov 1883

Ernest Cipriano SOTO [6]
Born 07 Sep 1899   #332
San Simeon, SLO Co., California
Marr 1923
San Luis Obispo Co., California
Died 31 Dec 1979
San Luis Obispo, California

Carmel Irene ASEBEZ
Born 23 May 1879   #207
San Simeon, SLO Co., California
Died 07 Apr 1964
San Luis Obispo, California

Giacomo BARLOGIO
Giacomo BARLOGIO   #1064

Rosa LUCHESSA
#1065

Vernon Ernest SOTO [7]
Born 17 Oct 1925   #593
Cambria, SLO Co., California
Marr 15 Mar 1945
San Luis Obispo Co., California

Giacomo BARLOGIO
Born 14 August 1868   #585
Gerra Piano,Ticino, Switzerland
Marr 24 Sep 1894
San Luis Obispo, California
Died 1941
San Luis Obispo Co., California

Carlo ANTOGNAZZI
#1062

Domenica TOGNAZZINI
#1063

Elsie L. BARLOGIO
Born 25 Sep 1905   #587
Cambria, SLO Co., California
Died 11 Feb 1989
Templeton, SLO Co., California

Angelica ANTOGNAZZI
Born 25 October 1866   #586
Riveo, Ticino, Switzerland
Died 1949
San Luis Obispo, California

Robert Vernon SOTO [8]
Born 27 Jun 1950   #602
San Luis Obispo Co., California
Marr 12 May 1979
Tioga, Hancock Co., Illinois
Spouse: Debra Mae "Debbie" GERHARDT

William SMITHERS
#2325

(unknown)
#2326

Amos J. SMITHERS
Born 31 Oct 1851   #2321
Woodstock, Ontario, Canada
Marr 14 Dec 1878
San Luis Obispo, California
Died 16 Jan 1933
Cambria, SLO Co., California

Samuel Newell TERRILL
Born 22 Sep 1822   #2219
Marr 14 Feb 1851
Died 30 Jun 1857

Roxana LEFFINGWELL
Born 02 May 1836   #2220
Died 29 Oct 1913

Lester E. SMITHERS
Born 23 Mar 1899   #670
Cambria, SLO Co., (twin)
Marr 30 Nov 1921
San Luis Obispo, California
Died 21 Apr 1938
Cambria, SLO Co., California

Ida Marcia TERRILL
Born 28 Nov 1856   #2322
Petaluma, Sonoma, California
Died 05 Sep 1914
Cambria, SLO Co., California

James Guess KESTER
Born abt 1844   #2327
Marr 20 Feb 1876
Died 25 Dec 1919

Mattie G. WALLACE
#2328

Althea L. SMITHERS
Born 12 Mar 1926   #600
San Luis Obispo Co., California

Edwin James KESTER
Born 01 Apr 1877   #2323
Cayucos, SLO Co., California
Marr 10 Nov 1901
Adelaida, SLO Co., California
Died 27 Dec 1957
Cambria, SLO Co., California

Gladys Althea KESTER
Born 25 Aug 1902   #671
Cambria, SLO Co., California
Died 03 Mar 1987
San Luis Obispo Co., California

Lucy F. McKEON
Born 1879   #2324
California
Died 1961
Cambria, SLO Co., California

Courtesy: Newell Terrill

Soto Family tree, page 1

27 Jun 2007

Jose Lazaro SOTO[3]
Born Dec 1801 #394
Mission San Antonio, California
Marr 16 Dec 1825
Mission San Carlos de, #937
Died ??
California

- **Isidro SOTO**[2]
  Born 05 Feb 1780 #406
  San Francisco, California
  Marr 21 Dec 1799
  Mission Santa Clara, #849
  Died Nov 1847
  San Juan Bautista, California

  - **Ygnacio de SOTO**[1]
    Born Feb 1749 #400
    Mocorito, Sinaloa, Mexico
    Marr abt 1773
    Villa de Sinaloa, Sinaloa, Mexico
    Died 23 Feb 1807
    San Jose, California
    - **Juan Nicolas de SOTO**
      #410
      Marr
    - **Maria Juliana de AVILA**
      #411

  - **Maria B. ESPINOSA**
    Born abt 1760 #401
    Villa de Sinaloa, Sinaloa, Mexico
    Died 31 Aug 1797
    San Jose, Calif.
    - **Joaquin ESPINOSA**
      Born abt 1710 #440
      Marr abt 1729
      Died ??
    - **Maria de LUGO**
      Born abt 1713 #441
      Died ??

- **Maria Marcela LINARES**
  Born 13 Dec 1777 #418
  San Francisco, California
  Died ??
  Alta California

  - **Ygnacio A. LINARES**
    Born abt 1745 #745
    San Miguel de, Mexico
    Marr abt 1767
    San Miguel de, Mexico
    Died 05 Jun 1805
    San Jose, California
    - **Gregorio LINARES**
      #1426
      Marr
    - **Manuela GONZALES**
      #1427

  - **Maria Gertrudis RIVAS**
    Born abt 1752 #746
    San Miguel de, Mexico
    Died 03 Dec 1813
    San Jose, California

General H. SOTO[4]
Born 11 Sep 1830 #300
San Juan Bautista, California
Marr abt 1869
Jolon, Monterey Co., California
Died 03 May 1906
Cambria, SLO Co., California
Spouse: Dolores GRAHALVA

Maria Felicita CANTUA
Born 05 Jul 1809 #303
San Juan Bautista, California
Died ??
California

- **Jose de G. CANTUA**
  Born 10 Dec 1786 #283
  Monterey, California
  Marr 09 Jan 1809
  Mission San Fernando Rey, #469
  Died aft 1870
  San Luis Obispo, California

  - **Ygnacio CANTUA**
    Born abt 1740 #334
    Navajoa, Sonora, Mexico
    Marr 1773
    Mexico
    Died Dec 1822
    Monterey, California

  - **Maria G. CASTILLO**
    Born abt 1760 #335
    Real de Santa Ana, Baja, Mexico
    Died bef 1822
    Monterey, California

- **Maria Petra M. LUGO**
  Born Jan 1787 #284
  Santa Barbara, California
  Died Mar 1817
  San Luis Obispo Co., California

  - **Luis Gonzaga LUGO**
    Born abt 1753 #346
    Loreto, Baja California, Mexico
    Marr abt 1786
    Mission de Santa Barbara
    Died May 1825
    Santa Barbara, California
    - **Francisco Ginez LUGO**
      #2240
      Marr abt 1750
    - **Maria G. ARMENTA**
      #2241

  - **Maria Antonia CAMPOS**
    Born abt 1758 #347
    Villa de Sinaloa, Sinaloa, Mexico
    Died 25 Jan 1791
    Santa Barbara, California

Courtesy: Newell Terrill

Soto Family tree, page 2

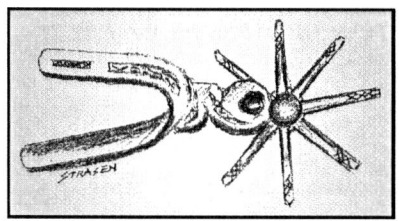

GENERATION 9 (MONTE)

Including Ygnacio Soto, who came to California at age twenty-six in 1775, Monte and Melissa are the ninth generation of California Sotos. Monte was born in 1982 and Melissa in 1984. Both children attended and graduated from Coast Union High school and then Cal Poly State University in December 2005. Monte has a degree in Bioresource and Agricultural Engineering; during college and after graduation he worked for EDA Design Professionals, a civil engineering company in San Luis

Courtesy: Robert Soto
Monte Soto horseback (on Rojo) at Home Ranch; 2001

Obispo. On July 8, 2006, Monte married his high school sweetheart, Kati Purchase of Cayucos.

Traditionally, the Soto family has been strictly Catholic in its religious affiliation, but more recent marriages to non-Catholic spouses has somewhat changed this. Monte and Kati's wedding took place at the Cambria Community Presbyterian Church, with the reception following at the ranch. The reception was a very special party, taking place on a beautiful day under the shade of the native oaks. There were some three hundred guests in attendance with an outdoor barbecue, drinks flowing, music by the Monte Mills band, and a wooden dance floor that was constantly full. Monte Mills commented it was one the best weddings they had ever played. The party lasted late into the night.

Monte seemed to excel at everything he did in high school. He received excellent grades, participated in sports, and always had many friends. Grandpa Vernon was very proud of Monte's football prowess. Because Monte was quick and fast, he was the running back for the offensive squad. The first time he touched the ball on an end-around sweep, he scored a touchdown. In his junior year, his football team won the Coast Sierra League and made it into the semifinal CIF round before finally being eliminated. Monte was also the point guard in basketball and played first base (being left-handed) in baseball. He was voted homecoming king in his senior year of 2001 at Coast Union High School.

He was also very successful in receiving scholarships while attending Cal Poly State University. He received four years' of California Farm Bureau scholarships, a Cattlewoman scholarship, and scholarships from the State Native Daughters and from the State Consulting Engineers and Land Surveyors Association. In Monte's fourth year at Poly (2005) he was voted "outstanding senior in the Agricultural Engineering program." In addition, he received recognition by becoming a member of the National Mortar Board Association.

In January 2008, Monte left EDA and began working for Cal Poly State University in the Irrigation Training and Research Center (ITRC). This new direction was very exciting for him because he has recently received his state PE (Professional Engineer) civil engineering license. Monte has since left Cal Poly employment and is working full time on the family cattle ranch. Monte is most proud of being a cowboy like all the Sotos before him.

Monte was a hard act for Melissa to follow, but she always looked up to her brother and was proud of his accomplishments. She also excelled in high school and graduated third in her class. She was very active in school, joining several organizations and becoming an officer in many of them. Melissa's greatest sports accomplishment was winning CIF in cross country. Because of this achievement her name graces a banner in the high school gym.

Melissa also went to Cal Poly State University and graduated in only three and a half years. She was able to complete school in such a short time by attending summer school. In her third year, she studied in Cuernavaca, Mexico, through a Cal Poly exchange program. This was an excellent experience for her, although it was hard because she missed her boyfriend and future husband, Tim Carstairs. Melissa worked at several jobs both during high school and while attending Cal Poly. It was because of her ambition and determination that she put herself through school.

Melissa graduated from Cal Poly with a degree in Liberal Studies, which provides a solid foundation for a teaching credential. After college, she worked full-time for Downey Savings. Her first full-time job required her to travel around the county and to work at various branches of Downey Savings. She was soon promoted to assistant branch manager in Arroyo Grande. She then began working as a loan officer, allowing her to be somewhat independent and to work out of her Paso Robles home. Early in 2008, Melissa began working for the University of Phoenix as an enrollment specialist. She has currently completed her master's degree and needs only her student-teaching requirement to receive her teaching credential.

On July 29, 2006, Melissa married Tim Carstairs in a unique garden wedding and reception held in our yard. Melissa and Tim were very pleased with this special event, which was attended by 125 family and friends. It was a beautiful evening, one highlighted by the gorgeous bride emerging from the formal front door of the living room and walking down several concrete steps to the ceremony held below on the lawn.

Courtesy: Marcia & Michael
Beautiful bride Melissa at garden wedding; 2006

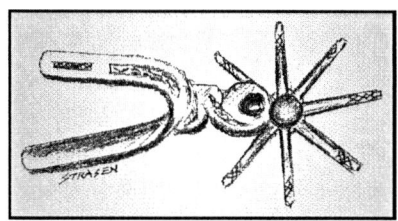

GENERATION 10 (RHETT)

In December of 2009, Monte and Katie welcomed a baby boy into this world. Rhett Monte Soto is a tenth-generation Californian who, we can hope, will appreciate his family background of a fledging and developing early-day California.

In May of 2007, Melissa and Tim had a baby girl named Mackenzie Mae Carstairs. She was born at French Hospital in San Luis Obispo and is

Courtesy: Kati Soto

Monte and Rhett on Derby

now also a rare tenth-generation California native. However, the most recent addition to the Soto family is Alina Mae Carstairs, a daughter born to Melissa and Tim in 2010. It is with great happiness that the Soto family can now continue a new generation in California history.

Courtesy: Robert Soto

Mackenzie, Melissa and Alina

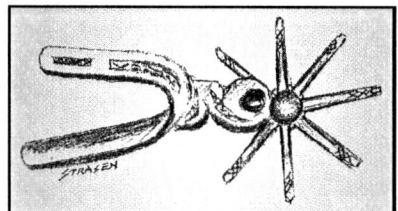

SUMMARY

It was very important for me to complete this book. I'm so appreciative of all prior family members who suffered through many hardships while settling this vast and primitive land. I can only imagine the difficulties involved in Ygnacio Soto's 1,500-mile excursion into Alta California in 1775. With little food and sparse water, bringing his family of two children and a pregnant wife through primitively charted territory is beyond comprehension. Leaving all traces and memories of your extended family members behind, and realizing you would never see or speak with any of them again, would have been nearly unbearable. Not knowing what fate awaited your family once you arrived at your destination would also prove disconcerting. Would Indians be friendly or would they be the savages everyone feared? These thoughts would only begin to envelop the uncertainties going through a person's mind. These feelings are surely what Ygnacio experienced.

Isidoro, also a military soldier, would be next. His life span would include the period of rapid growth of Spanish influence in the area to the beginnings of the Anglo influences. It would encompass the romantic period of the Spanish and then Mexican ranchos. Lifestyles were proud; horsemanship was essential and considered the only means to accomplish work. It would also be during Isidoro's lifetime that Spain would lose its hold and Mexico would take political control of the desirable California.

Next would be Lazaro, who witnessed the influx of the forty-niners and the effects of Manifest Destiny. These two changes would bring an end to the romantic period of the "Dons" along with their lifestyle. Gone were the days of a handshake being your bond and word. Now everything was legalized by written contract only, English was the chosen language, and California was part of the United States of America. Everything had changed in three short generations. Californios who were once considered respectful, honest, and hard-working people were shoved aside in their own land. There was no loyalty, morals had deteriorated, and the influx of miners and settlers overran their beloved country. The Californios had become outcasts in their own society.

General Soto would live through all these changes too. It would be during General's life that the great ranchos would be dismembered, forcing him into isolation from Anglo authority by moving into a remote place. However, this proved impossible since Anglo influences were felt everywhere. Land would be "legally" stolen from General, leaving a very bitter taste of anything to do with the new white culture. Although he later homesteaded in the nearby Adelaida area, General would be the first Soto to move to the Cambria area. He made a great effort to continue practicing his forefather's customs and traditions. Family was always considered primary, with proper respect given to everyone.

Cipriano would be the first of the Sotos to be heavily influenced by Anglo culture on a day-to-day basis. He would be forced to learn English in order to find employment. Spanish would now be spoken only at home, never in public. Cipriano worked for the Hearst family his entire career and was highly respected because of his proud heritage and mannerisms. When Cipriano spoke, even when using his soft tone, everyone listened because it was important.

Ernest was the next Soto to assimilate into the Anglo culture by working at Hearst Castle after it was acquired by the State of California. However, he continued the family tradition of raising cattle and working the land. Ernest would be the first Soto to marry outside the Spanish-Mexican culture, with his wife, Elsie, being of Swiss descent.

As his grandfather Cipriano did, Vernon also worked for the Hearst Ranch as a vaquero-cowboy and in addition earned a living as a cattle rancher. He also married outside the Hispanic culture, with his wife, Althea, being of English descent and from one of the early Cambria families (Leffingwell). Vernon was the first of the Sotos to speak English only. The Soto family was now Anglicized and fully immersed into its culture. The once dark-skinned people were now pale, with only memories of family members gone long before them.

I now carry only a trace of the once-proud blood originating in Spain over three hundred and fifty years ago. Continuing to work at Hearst Castle until my retirement in 2003, I have led a life immersed in Anglo culture. Gone are many of the family traditions of the past. But I was also raised to live honestly and to treat everyone with respect. I look back into my past and feel the presence of all my forefathers. It is now understood how they lived and what drove them to their way of life. The pure love of the land with its natural beauty is paramount in my mind, but family is considered first priority; it is all that truly matters in life. The essence of life is acknowledged through our children; it is the greatest accomplishment we can pass down to make a better existence for all. Family is our true legacy.

It is these feelings that directed me to write this book, to explain the Soto family in early California, to document our family stories, and to make sense of history.

BIBLIOGRAPHY

Acuña, Rodolfo F. *Occupied America: A History of Chicanos.* New York: Harper & Row, 1981. Reprinted 2004.

Adams, Carol. Oral history of Margaret and Lila Soto. Cambria. May 9, 1985.

Alarcon, Norma, et al. *Chicano Critical Issues.* Berkeley: Third Woman Press, 1993.

Angel, Myron. *History of San Luis Obispo County, California, with Illustrations and Biographical Sketches of Its Prominent Men and Pioneers.* Oakland: Thompson & West, 1883.

Anonymous. "An Account of a Voyage on San Francisco Bay; By Captain John Greer. Sunday, January 13th, 1850" article in *The Californians* magazine, Vol. 11, No.5, date unknown.

Anonymous. "Ernest Soto Grand Marshal of 25th Pinedorado Parade" article in *The Cambrian,* June 7, 1973.

Anonymous. "Lesson Stays with Former Merchant" article in *The Cambrian,* July 10, 1997.

Anonymous. "Juan Soto" article in the *San Francisco Chronicle,* May 15, 1874. Reprinted June 3, 1934.

Anonymous. "Ed Terrill Accident" article in the *San Luis Obispo Tribune,* October 29, 1915.

Anonymous. "San Simeon Bay" article in the *San Luis Obispo Tribune,* October 26, 1883.

Baker, Gayle. *Cambria.* Santa Barbara: Harbor Town Histories, 2003.

Bancroft, Herbert. "California Pioneer Register and Index: 1542–1848." In Bancroft's *History of California.* San Francisco: A.L. Bancroft, 1884-1890. Seven Vols.

Beebe, Rose Marie, and Robert M. Senkewicz, eds. *Lands of Promise and Despair.* Berkeley: Heyday Books, 2001.

Beebe, Rose Marie, and Robert M. Senkewicz, *Testimonios: Early California through the Eyes of Women: 1815–1848.* Berkeley: Heyday Books, 2006.

Burciaga, Jose Antonio. *Drink Cultura: Chicanismo.* Santa Barbara: Capra Press, 1993.

Cambria Historical Society. *The Brambles*. Cambria. August, 2008.

Chavez-Garcia, Miroslava. "Mexican Women and the American Conquest in Los Angeles." Doctoral dissertation. Ann Arbor, Michigan: University Microfilms International, 1999.

Conley, Frances. *Long Road to Rancho San Pablo*. Oakland: East Bay Blue Print, 1989.

Conmy, Peter Thomas. "The Native Son." Article in unknown Magazine, Vol. 29, No.4, December 1989-January 1990.

Crosby, Harry W. *Gateway to California*. San Diego: Sunbelt Publications, 2003.

Davis, William Heath. *Seventy-Five Years in California*. San Francisco: John Howell Books, 1929/1967.

Fink, Augusta. *Monterey County: The Dramatic story of Its Past*. Santa Cruz: Western Tanager Press, 1972.

Garate, Don. *Juan Bautista de Anza: National Historic Trail*. Tucson: Southwest Parks and Monuments Association, 1994.

Guerrero, Vladimir. *The Anza Trail and the Settling of California*. Berkeley: Heyday Books, 2006.

Hachigian, Michelle. Courtesy of Hearst Castle®/California State Parks. Oral history interview of Archie Soto, Cayucos, May 26, 1976.

Hamilton, Geneva. *Where the Highway Ends*. Cambria: Williams Printing Company, 1974.

Hanchett, Byron. *In & Around the Castle*. San Luis Obispo: Blake Publishing, 1985.

Heneken, Nellie Imwalle. "It Happened Like This…" article in *Monterey Bay News*. Seaside, California. July 9, 1948.

Ingles, Beth. "Title Finally Cleared After 90 Years of Litigation" article in *The Monterey Peninsula Herald*. Monterey, March 23, 1943.

Johnson, Rodney. "Famed Encounter Between Miller and Vasquez Took Place in a Local Barroom" article in *San Luis Obispo Telegram-Tribune*, May 8, 1956.

McCleary, John. *"Bandits, Ghosts and a Nobel Prize Winner Have Slept Here"* pamphlet from City of Monterey, Monterey Institute of International Studies. Monterey. Not dated.

MacGillivray, J. Fraser *The Story of Adelaida*. Paso Robles and San Luis Obispo: Privately Published, 1992.

MacLean, Angus. *Legends of the California Banditos.* Fresno: Pioneer Publishing, 1977.

Margolin, Malcolm. *Monterey in 1786: The Journals of Jean Francois De La Persouse.* Berkeley: Heyday Books. 1989.

Margolin, Malcolm. *Preserving the Layers of History.* Berkeley: Heyday Books, 1997.

Mason, William Marvin. *The Census of 1790: A Demographic History of Colonial California.* Menlo Park: Ballena Press, 1998.

Mora, Jo. *Californios.* New York: Doubleday & Company, Inc., 1949.

Mora-Torres, Gregorio, ed. *Californio Voices: The Oral Memoirs of Jose Maria Amador and Lorenzo Asisara.* Based on manuscripts originally recorded by Thomas Savage in 1877. Denton, Texas: University of North Texas Press, 2005.

Morrison, Annie L. and John H. Haydon, *History of San Luis Obispo County and Environs.* Los Angeles: Historic Record Company, 1917.

Northrop, Marie E. *Spanish–Mexican Families of Early California: 1769–1850.* New Orleans: Polyanthos, 1976.

O'Donnell, Mayo Hayes. "Joaquin Soto's Will" article in the *Monterey Peninsula Herald.* February 1, 1951.

Ohles, Wallace V. *The Lands of Mission San Miguel.* Fresno: Word Dancer Press, 1997.

Oppel, Frank. *Tales of Old California.* Secaucus, New Jersey: Castle Books, 1989.

Osio, Antonio Maria. *The History of Alta California-A Memoir of Mexican California.* Rose Marie Beebe and Robert M. Senkewicz, eds. Madison, Wisconsin: The University of Wisconsin Press, 1996.

Pitt, Leonard. *The Decline of the Californios.* Berkeley: University of California Press, 1966.

Pourade, Richard F. *Anza Conquers the Desert: The Anza Expeditions from Mexico to California and the Founding of San Francisco, 1774 to 1776.* San Diego: Union–Tribune Publishing Co., 1971.

Rademacker, Francis. Oral History Tape of the Soto Family. Cambria. 1954.

Reinstedt, Randall A. *Ghosts, Bandits and Legends of Old Monterey.* Carmel: Ghost Town Publications, 1974.

Rosenus, Alan. *General M. G. Vallejo and the Advent of the Americans.* Albuquerque: University of New Mexico Press, 1995.

Secrest, William B. *California Desperadoes: Stories of Early California Outlaws in Their Own Words.* Clovis: Word Dancer Press, 2000.

Sepulveda, Bartolome. "Noticias Para Los Californianos." Article in Unknown Magazine, Volume 8, Number 2. March-April 1976.

Shinn, Charles Howard. *Pioneer Spanish Families in California.* Santa Barbara: W. T. Genns, 1896.

Smith, Margarita Griggs. *The San Simeon Story.* San Luis Obispo: Star-Reporter Publishing Co., 1958.

Soto, Shirlene. Oral History of Ernest Soto. Cambria, January 29 and February 5, 1978.

Squibb, Paul. Notes from Dry Bones Trip of 7/8/1961. Cambria, July 8, 1961.

Squibb, Paul. Oral Interview of Joaquin (Jack) Soto. Cambria. July 1 and July 4, 1957.

Squibb, Paul. Oral Interview of Loren (Lowell) Thorndyke. Cambria. August 5, 1965.

Thompson & West. *History of San Luis Obispo County, California.* 1883. Reprint. Fresno: Valley Publishers, 1979.

Vigil, Sam Jr. "A Long Line of Sotos." *The Cambria-San Simeon Country News.* December 17–23, 1980.

Williams, Delmar. *Chronicles of Cambria's Pioneers.* Cambria: Marcus Waltz, 1946.

INDEX

Aceves, Antonio 18
Acuna, Professor Rodolfo 33
Adams, Carol 10
Alarcón, Norma 24
Allen, George 78
Altamirano, Justo Roberto 19
Alvarado, Juan Bautista 37, 39, 48, 58
Alvarez, Luis 18
Alviso, Domingo 19
Alviso, Jose Maria 62
Alviso, Maria Antonia 27
Amador, Jose Maria 25
Amesquita, Juana Maria 27
Amezquita, Juan 19
Antognazzi, Carlo 171
Anza, Juan Bautista 9, 12-16, 18, 20, 22-23
Anza, Juan Bautista (Sr.) 14
Archuleta, Maria 62
Arellano, Manuel 19
Argeullo, Captain Don Luis Antonio 25
Arguello, Alferez Jose Dario 27, 49
Armenta, Maria G. 172
Arques, Joaquin 68
Arrieta, Maria Rita Quiteria 50
Asabez, Frank "Ponch" 75, 76, 117
Asabez, Raymond 113, 114
Asebez, Anastasio 4, 87, 90, 91, 171
Asebez, Anna 87
Asebez, Clara 4, 87
Asebez, Edward 4, 79, 87, 88, 91-93, 109, 113, 115, 119, 120
Asebez, Erlinda 87
Asebez, Josefa 4, 87, 109
Asebez, Placida (Garcia) 87, 114, 171
Asisara, Lorenzo 25, 26
Atherton, Faxon Dean 46, 69, 70
Bancroft, Herbert 24, 29, 45, 47
Barba, Morie 79, 113
Barlogio, Angelica (Antognazzi) 128, 171
Barlogio, Edmondo 113, 114, 154, 166
Barlogio, Giacomo 171
Barlogio, James 128, 132, 171
Bassi, Mary 110

Bassi, Olivia 110, 111, 113
Bassi, Sylvia 110
Beebe, Rose Marie 26, 29, 37, 39
Bernal, Juan Francisco 18, 19
Bernal, Maria Josefa 18
Berreyesa, Maria de la Luz Ines 28
Biaggini, Ed Jr. 81
Bianchini, James 113, 114, 118
Blake, "Boots" 159
Blanch, Josephine 53
Bojorges, Gerardo 61
Bojorques, Pedro 19
Bojorques, Ramon 19
Bojorquez, Maria Ana Antonia 28, 31
Bolcoff, Jose Antonio 26
Borradori, Sam 139
Boronda, Maria Teresa 28
Botts, Jack 130
Botts, Joe 75, 130
Bouchard, Hipolito 39
Bowen, Arthur 46
Bright, Mabel 80, 81
Bucarelli, Viceroy 15, 22
Buelna, Antonio 58, 62
Buffum, James Monroe 132
Burciago, Jose Antonio 32, 33
Butrino, Maria Antonia 27
Butron, Maria Juana Lorenza 28
Camozzi, Ethel 158
Campos, Maria Antonia 172
Cantua, Jose Guadalupe 31, 45, 172
Cantua, Josie 114
Cantua, Juan Bautista 31
Cantua, Julian 42
Cantua, Maria Felicita 31, 37, 45, 172
Cantua, Maria Guadalupe 31
Cantua, Vicente 25, 26
Cantua, Ygnacio 31, 172
Caravajales, Jose Maria 78
Carstairs, Alina 178
Carstairs, Mackenzie 177, 178
Carstairs, Melissa (Soto) 10, 161, 166, 167, 173, 175-178

Carstairs, Tim 175, 177, 178
Cassanova, Rev. Angelo 55
Castillo, Maria Gertrudis 31, 172
Castro, Esteram 68
Castro, Francisco 36
Castro, Gabriela 36
Castro, J.A. 30
Castro, Joaquin 19
Castro, Juan 68
Castro, Maria del Carmen 36, 37, 47, 53, 65, 68
Castro, Mariano 65
Castro, Pablo Antonio Maria 36
Chavez-Garcia, Miroslava 48
Chavoya, Antonio 62
Chavoya, Cruz 61
Chavoya, Pedro 62
Clark, Captain Joseph 94
Clausen, Bill 85
Coffman, Janis 8, 9
Coffman, Taylor 8, 9, 10
Conley, Frances 17, 35
Cooksey, Ben 4
Cooksey, Elmer 4
Copeland, Dennis 51
Copinger, John 58
Copinger, Manuela 59
Costillo, Maria Gertrudis 31
Cota, Juan 30
Crosby, Harry 15
Davis, Marian 81, 85
Davis, William Heath 24
de Arrillaga, Jose Joaquin 27
de Avila, Maria Juliana 13, 172
de Galvez, Jose 13, 14
de Neve, Felipe 16
Dutra, Antonio 51
Dutra, Ramona 51
Ebline, Charlie 139
Elliott, Walter 161
Espinosa, Joaquin 172
Estanislao, [Indian] 26, 27
Estenaga, Father Tomas 48
Estrada, Francisco "Pancho" 78, 110, 147
Estrada, Joaquin 68

Estrada, Julian 68
Evans, Ed 111, 112
Evans, Helen 111
Fages, Pedro 15
Farrari, Elmo 155
Felicita, [Indian] 68
Felix, Vicente 19
Fernandez, Jose 63
Fink, Augusta 70
Fiscalini, Alfred 153
Fiscalini, Constantine 151
Fiscalini, Eddie 168
Fiscalini, Louis 128
Fiscalini, Olympio 151
Fiscalini, Olympio "Olie" Jr. 153, 168
Fitzhugh, Abbott 139
Fitzhugh, Dee 81, 136, 137, 139
Fitzhugh, Elmer 139
Fitzhugh, Mrs. Caroline 139
Fitzhugh, Minabelle 81
Fitzhugh, Will Thomas 139
Flores, Teodoro 62
Fremont, John C. 32, 67
Gallegos, Carlos 19
Garate, Don 12
Garcia, Antonio 18
Garcia, Celestino 78
Garcia, Cora 114
Garcia, Ed 113, 114
Garcia, Francisco Maria 28
Garcia, Jose de la Luz 28
Garcia, Manuel 30
Garcia, Salvador 62
Gerhardt, Gary 168
Gerhardt, Kathleen (Fiscalini) 168
Gerhardt, Wayne 168
Gernardini, Roy 93, 94
Gonzales, Manuela 172
Goodall, Boberta 158
Goodall, Mrs. 81
Grahalva, John 91
Green, Maria (Littlejohn) 68, 69
Green, Samuel 68, 69
Greene, Mary L. 56
Greer, Captain John 58-60

Greer, Lucas 59-61
Grijalva, Sergeant Juan 19
Guerrero, Vladimir 17
Gunther, Lee 113
Gutierrez, Ygnacio 18
Hake, Mike 167
Hamilton, Geneva 9, 77
Hanchett, Byron 107
Hartzell, William "Bill" 150
Haydon, John 68, 91
Health, Dr. Scott 56
Hearst, George 69, 82, 90, 98
Hearst, Patty 169
Hearst, Pheobe Apperson 89, 90, 98, 107, 109
Hearst, William Randolph 69, 101, 109
Heneken, Nellie Imwalle 54
Henry I, King of England 12
Henry IV, King of England 12
Hernandez, Maria Trinidad 27, 52
Higuera, Ana Maria Antonia 25, 27, 36
Higuera, Jose Joaquin 28
Higuera, Pantaleón 26
Hitchcock, Ed 115
How Wong 152, 153
Ingles, Verl "Giggs" 127
Ingles, Beth 64
Ingles, Doris 109, 118, 139
Ingles, Levita 95, 113, 114, 118
Ingles, Reno "Dad" 95, 101, 113, 118
Jack, Christine 80
Johnson, Rodney 38
Jones, Commodore Thomas ap Catesby 32
Junge, Lloyd 159
Kester, Edwin "Ed" 156, 171
Kester, James Guess 171
Kester, Lucy (McKeon) 156, 171
Kreiger, Dan 101
Langley, Neil 167
Lara y Zabala, Maria de Jesús 51
Lara, Dona Feliciana 51
Leffingwell, Roxana Matilda 156, 171
Lehman, John 136
Lehman, Louisa 136, 137
Leimert, Walter 155

Lesse, Don Luis 65
Lewis, Billy 146
Linares, Gregorio 172
Linares, Maria Marcela 27, 29, 37, 64, 172
Linares, Ygnacio Antonio 19, 29, 172
Lopez, Sebastián 19
Lownes, BJ 158
Lowry, Bob 154
Lowry, Carol (Soto) 10, 106, 113, 114, 145, 154
Lowry, John 75
Lucchessa, Rosa 171
Lugo (de Lugo), Francisco Ginez 172
Lugo (de Lugo), Francisco Salvador 18
Lugo (de Lugo), Maria Antonia Isabela 18
Lugo (de Lugo), Maria Petra M. 172
Lugo, Luis Gonzaga 172
Lugo, Petra Maxima 31, 45, 172
Lyons, Hazel 9
Lyons, Wilford 9, 134
MacGillivray, J. Fraser 156
MacLean, Angus 34
Margolin, Malcolm 46, 49
Marks, Miles C. 69
Marquart, Estelle 131, 134
Marquart, John 131, 132, 134, 139, 147
Martin, Dennis 59
Martinez, Mariano 62
Mayfield, Frank 78
McCleary, John 53
McKinley, President William 71
McMillan, Mr. 139
Mesa, Jose Dolores 61
Mesa, Juan 28
Mesa, Maria Antonia 28, 57, 58, 61, 63
Mesa, Valerio 19
Messic, Lilly 79 113, 114, 118
Micheltorena, Manuel 37, 48
Miller, Henry 38
Mills, Monte 174
Mora, Alphonzio Tobias "Bias" 139
Mora, Jo 30
Mora, Laurence 114, 139
Mora, Lilly 113
Mora, Rafael 80, 113-115

INDEX

Moraga, Lieutentant Joaquin 19, 27
Morano, Theresa 92
Mora-Torres 25
Moreno, Pedro 78
Moreno, Rafael 62
Morrison, Annie 68, 91
Morse, Sheriff 35
Murphy, Lillian 132
Murrieta, Joaquin 30, 34, 35, 38
Murrieta, Tomas 34
Nieto, Juana Maria Perez 48
Noriega, Jose 63
Northrop, Marie 18
O'Donnell, Mayo Hayes 46
Ohles, Wallace 36, 49
Olivares, Bonifacio 65
Olmsted, Hazel 137
Olmsted, Rufus Burnett 68, 73, 137
Oppel, Frank 44
Ortega, Ignacio 39-41, 43
Osio, Antonio 37
Osio, Antonio Maria 37
Osio, Beatriz 37
Osio, Jose Antonio 37
Osio, Jose Manuel 37
Osio, Juan de la Cruz 37
Osorio, Eveline 70
Pacheco, Bartolome Ygnacio 27
Pacheco, Juan 19
Pacheco, Maria Petra 28
Pacheco, Salvio 63
Palou, Father Francisco 24
Pastor, Ygnacio 69
Pavlik, Robert 10
Pena, Jose 58
Peralta, Gabriel 19
Pico, Pio 32
Pico, Santiago 19
Pinto, Pablo 19
Pitt, Leonard 32, 36, 73
Portola (de Portola), Gaspar 15, 22
Pourade, Richard 22
Pujol, Domingo 68
Quijada, Maria Rosalia 50
Rademacker, Francis "Franie" 75, 110

Radford, Milene 10
Rambo, Gene 148
Randall, Andrew 46
Reali, Joe 117
Redendo, Thomas 34
Reinstedt, Randall 30
Reis, Eddie 95
Reis, Frank 95
Reis, Joe 95
Reis, Johnny 95, 146
Ricardo, Juan 68
Rivas, Gertrudis 29, 172
Rivera (de Rivera), Captain Fernando 18
Roach, Sheriff 64, 65
Robles, "El Chato" 25
Robles, Abelino 25, 26
Robles, Jose de la Luz 28
Robles, Nicolas 25
Robles, Secundino 25
Rodríguez, Damaso Antonio 28
Rodriquez, Jesus 162
Rogers, Will 130
Romero, Concepcion 62
Romero, Josefa 65
Romero, Mrs. Juan 57
Rosas, Manuel 78
Rotanzi, Norman 129
Ruiz, Maria Jacinta 31
Sanchez, Jose 19
Sanchez, Jose Antonio 28
Sanchez, Juana Maria Lorenza 37
Sanchez, Second Lieutenant 25
Schutz, Mony [sic] 98
Seale, Henry 60
Seale, Thomas 60
Sebastian, Pete 88
Senkewicz, Robert M. 26, 29, 37, 39
Sepulveda, Bartolomé 27
Serra, Father Junipero 15, 16, 22
Shinn, Charles 23
Sloat, Commodore John Drake 67
Smith, Margarita Griggs 97, 99, 100
Smithers, Amos 155, 156, 171
Smithers, Eldon 157, 160
Smithers, Ernest "Friday" 159

Smithers, Ervin 157
Smithers, Gladys (Kester) 155, 171
Smithers, Lester 155, 156, 171
Smithers, Lester Jr. "Dutch" 155, 157-160
Smithers, Marlene 157, 160
Smithers, Shirley 157, 159, 160
Smithers, William 171
Smithers, William "Bill" 157, 160
Snow, Karen (Soto) 10
Soberanes, Francisco 51
Soria, Avelina "Lilly" 70, 71
Sotelo, Jose 19
Soto (de Soto), Alejandro 15
Soto (de Soto), Jose Antonio 13, 18, 27
Soto (de Soto), Juan Nicolas 13, 172
Soto (de Soto), Maria Antonia Francisca 13, 18, 27
Soto (de Soto), Mateo Ignacio 15
Soto (deSoto), Ygnacio 12, 13, 16-18, 22-24, 26, 27, 29, 31, 37, 44, 49, 61, 172, 173, 179
Soto Augustine "Count" 53-56, 65
Soto Felicida 51
Soto, Agnes (Maggetti) 79, 80, 84, 85, 113, 115-118, 122, 156
Soto, Althea (Smithers) 8, 10, 31, 112-114, 140, 150, 155-164, 166, 171
Soto, Andrew 4, 87, 91, 93, 97, 101, 104, 109-111, 113, 118, 127, 128, 135, 138, 140, 151, 152, 154
Soto, Andrew Jr. "Snow" 10, 96, 113, 114, 118, 142, 143, 150-152
Soto, Antonio 13, 26, 27
Soto, Archie 4, 101-103, 113, 114, 118, 129, 139, 142
Soto, Augustine 65
Soto, Augustine "Gus" 79, 109, 110, 113, 114, 118, 135, 138, 143
Soto, Barbara 65
Soto, Bernardino 65, 68, 69
Soto, Bernardino "Barney" 4, 77, 79, 88, 97-102, 113-115, 118, 132, 136-139, 143, 147, 156
Soto, Bonnie (Whitlock) 150, 152
Soto, Braulia 75, 79, 113

Soto, Calista 136
Soto, Candido (Ramon) 50
Soto, Carmel (Asebez) 3, 4, 31, 79, 87-91, 94, 98, 103-107, 109-114, 118, 126, 144, 171
Soto, Casilda 48
Soto, Cipriano 3, 4, 10, 31, 71, 79, 86-94, 96-99, 101, 103, 104, 106-114, 118, 119, 126, 138, 139, 143, 144, 147, 152, 170, 171, 180
Soto, Damisio 27
Soto, Debra (Gerhardt) 1, 31, 161, 165-169
Soto, Dolores (Grajalva) 4, 31, 50, 71, 75, 76, 79, 87, 91, 92, 119, 120, 122, 124, 171
Soto, Dona 134, 135
Soto, Edwin 101, 103, 113, 114, 118, 132
Soto, Elsie (Barlogio) 10, 31, 74, 88, 96, 97, 112, 118, 126-128, 131, 132, 134, 135, 138-140, 142, 143, 146, 154, 161, 166, 171
Soto, Ernest 10, 31, 74, 83, 88, 89, 91, 93, 110, 115, 118, 125-132, 135, 138-140, 143, 146, 151, 154, 170, 171, 180
Soto, Estevan 61, 63
Soto, Eugenio Antonio 23
Soto, Evelyn 88, 113, 114, 118, 143
Soto, Felipe 61
Soto, Francisco 13, 24-27, 36, 37, 52, 57
Soto, Francisco de las Llagas 61, 63
Soto, Francisco Maria 27
Soto, General Herculeano 4, 31, 46, 50, 66-71, 73-80, 82, 83, 87, 89, 91, 100, 122-124, 171, 172, 180
Soto, George "Chap" 135, 136
Soto, Guadalupe Epifanio 50
Soto, Guillermo 48, 49
Soto, Isidoro 27, 29, 30, 36, 37, 45, 46, 64, 172, 179
Soto, Jesús 51, 52
Soto, Jim 10, 78, 79, 89, 95, 104, 107, 113, 134, 139, 143, 144
Soto, Joaquin 25, 26, 36, 37, 45-47, 53, 64, 65, 68
Soto, Joaquin "Jack" 4, 10, 34, 53, 69, 74, 76, 77, 79-85, 88, 89, 113, 115-117, 118, 121, 123, 124, 137, 138, 143, 156
Soto, Joaquin Jr. "Pico" 9, 103, 116, 117

Index

Soto, Joe 4, 70, 71
Soto, Jose Guadalupe 61, 63
Soto, Jose Isidoro 50
Soto, Jose Joaquin 28
Soto, Jose M. 46
Soto, Jose Maria 65
Soto, Jose Ygnacio 51
Soto, Josefa 65
Soto, Juan Antonio 28
Soto, Juan [Outlaw] 30, 34, 35
Soto, Juan Capistrano 61, 63
Soto, Juan Crisostomo 61, 63
Soto, Katie (Purchase) 10, 174
Soto, Lazaro 31, 37, 45, 46, 67, 71, 172, 179
Soto, Lazaro 65
Soto, Lila 117, 124
Soto, Lilly (Messic) 79, 113
Soto, Luisa 65
Soto, Louisa "Beva" (Asabez) 4, 77, 79, 82, 91-93, 109, 119
Soto, Lucylle (Wagner) 87, 113, 114, 118
Soto, Manuel 51, 52
Soto, Manuel (Joaquin) 50
Soto, Margaret (Ingles) 79, 97-101, 113, 115, 118, 136, 137, 156
Soto, Margaret "Dolly" 10, 53, 116, 117, 124, 137
Soto, Maria Ana Josefa 28
Soto, Maria Barbara (Espinosa) 13, 18, 23, 24, 61, 172
Soto, Maria Barbara Rufina 36
Soto, Maria Bernarda 28
Soto, Maria Dolores 61, 63
Soto, Maria de Jesús 61, 63
Soto, Maria Eduviges 50
Soto, Maria Fernandia 28
Soto, Maria Francisca Cecilia 61, 63
Soto, Maria Josefa "Gertrudis" 50
Soto, Maria Juliana Angela Amanda 50
Soto, Maria Longina Celestina 50
Soto, Maria Luisa 57-61, 63
Soto, Maria Rafaela 28
Soto, Mariano Miguel Cipriano 50
Soto, Mary (Warren) 79, 135

Soto, Mary Francisca 79
Soto, Monica Ascensión 50
Soto, Monte 10, 161, 166, 167, 173-175, 177
Soto, Murial (Gillespie) 103, 113, 114, 118, 142
Soto, Narcisa Florencia 37
Soto, Pedro 65
Soto, Rafael 28, 44, 57, 58, 61
Soto, Ramon 45
Soto, Refugio 65
Soto, Rhett 178
Soto, Rita (Minetti) 103, 113, 114, 118
Soto, Robert "Bobby" 3, 8, 9, 31, 154, 161, 163-171, 180, 181
Soto, Shirlene 3, 10, 89, 96, 97, 126, 161, 162
Soto, Steven 10, 152
Soto, Teresa "Terri" 103
Soto, Theresa 136
Soto, Tomas Antonio 28
Soto, Vernon 8, 10, 31, 74, 96, 112-115, 131, 140-142, 144-146, 148, 150, 153-155, 161-164, 166, 170, 171, 174, 180
Soto, Violet (Ingles) 87, 101, 118, 127, 143
Souza, Johnny 139
Souza, Tilly 139
Spooner, Alden Bradford 75
Spooner, Ed 75, 79, 82
Spooner, Roxana 75
Squibb, Louise 80, 81, 84
Squibb, Paul 69, 74, 76, 80, 81, 84, 85, 93
Stanger, F.M. 61
Starkie, Alf 85
Steinbeck, John 53
Strassen, Bill 10, 16, 21, 99
Summers, Roy 94, 127
Sunol, Antonio 62
Taboas, Don Maximo 65
Tapia, Felipe 18
Taylor, Captain Murray 98, 101
Terrill, Arthur 4, 97, 109-111, 113
Terrill, Edward "Eddie" 4, 109, 119, 120
Terrill, Ida Marcia 156, 171
Terrill, Newell 10, 12, 47, 111
Terrill, Newell E. 109

Terrill, Oliver "Obie" 111, 113
Terrill, Samuel Newell 156, 171
Thompson, Glen 113
Thorndyke, Captain 95
Thorndyke, Clara Erma (Rogers) 96
Thorndyke, Cyril 139
Thorndyke, John Emery "Em" 96
Thorndyke, Lorin "Lowell" 93, 95, 96
Thorndyke, Maud (Rogers) 95
Tognazzini, Domenica 171
Truman, Major Benjamín 33
Valdez, Dorotea 29
Valencia, Jose 19
Valenzuela, Agustine 18
Vallejo, Mariano de Guadalupe 18, 32, 44
Vallejo, Jose Jesús 24
Van Ness, James 69
Vasquez, Dolores 62
Vasquez, Jose Hermenegildo 31
Vasquez, Juan 18, 31
Vasquez, Maria Concepción 53
Vasquez, Maria Rosalia 23, 28, 31
Vasquez, Tiburcio 30-33, 38, 53
Vasquez, Tiburcio (Sr.) 27, 31
Villa, Jose M. 65
Villavicencio, Maria Josefa 61
Wagnon, Doug 167
Wallace, Mattie G. 171
Wallace, Mr. 101
Warren, George 139
Warren, Will 139
Washburn, Hulda 154
Wentz. Mrs. 81
White, Sybil 113, 114
Williams, Betty (Soto) 113, 114, 116, 117, 124, 158
Williams, Delmar 72, 137
Williams, Howard 114
Yguera, Estevan 61